HOW TO
TEACH THE BIBLE

Lucien E. Coleman, Jr.

BROADMAN PRESS
Nashville, Tennessee

Quotations marked RSV are from the Revised Standard Version of the Bible, copyrighted 1946, 1952, © 1971, 1973.

Quotations marked TEV are from the *Good News Bible*, the Bible in Today's English Version. Old Testament: Copyright © American Bible Society 1976: New Testament: Copyright © American Bible Society 1966, 1971, 1976. Used by permission.

4234-28
ISBN: 0-8054-3428-3

Dewey Decimal Classification: 220.07
Subject heading: BIBLE-STUDY AND TEACHING
Library of Congress Catalog Card Number: 79-52001
Printed in the United States of America

To the memory of
Beulah Coleman
and
Mattie Holland,
faithful teachers of the Word

Contents

About This Book . . .

Some people will tell you that teachers are born, not made. Don't believe it. Teachers are born, all right. But as C. B. Eavey once quipped, "they aren't born made."

The ability to teach isn't some magical endowment buried in the chromosomes of a favored few. Teaching is a craft. It can be learned, practiced, and cultivated like any other high-level skill.

Unfortunately, many volunteer teachers in the church have never had the opportunity to learn, practice, and cultivate teaching skills. In a church just outside of Washington, D.C., for instance, a bright young woman handed me this note at the beginning of a weekend Bible-teaching clinic:

"I have never taught anything or anybody . . . . I don't know where to begin. Can you help?"

She wasn't alone in her dilemma. I meet many like her in churches large and small. Called upon to be teachers, they do the best they can; but they have serious doubts about their ability to do the job.

They ask the same questions over and over again:

• "How can I learn enough about the Bible to have something worth sharing with my class?"

• "Is there any way for a teacher to get members of her class involved in the lesson so she won't have to do all the talking?"

• "How do you interest people in Bible study when they seem to be totally indifferent to it?"

- "How do you get class members to study their lessons?"
- "How does one lead class members to do something about the message of the Bible, other than just sit there and listen to it?"
- "Where can I find out more about teaching methods?"
- "How do you prepare a teaching plan?"

The men and women asking such questions care deeply about Bible teaching. They want to do a good job, but they don't quite know how to go about it. That's why this book was written.

Some church teachers find help at summer conferences and various kinds of religious education workshops. In these settings they explore the nature of learning and teaching, talk about mutual problems, and try out new teaching skills. They often go back to their churches with their enthusiasm for Bible teaching rekindled.

But I keep thinking about the hundreds of volunteer teachers in the church who have never had an opportunity to attend even one Bible-teaching workshop. Some do well enough on their own initiative. But many are like Dave who came into the adult men's class in a small church two Sundays ago and said, "I hope you'll bear with me. I've been asked to take over this class. I told them that I didn't know anything about teaching, but they said there wasn't anybody else to take the job. I'll do the best I can, but I'll need your prayers."

There's no reason why Dave can't become a good Bible teacher, eventually. He is intelligent and personable, and he has a keen interest in Bible study. The problem is, no one has ever told him how to be a teacher. So he tries to muddle through, imitating what he has seen teachers before him do in class. He could really benefit from a good workshop in Bible teaching. But I doubt seriously that he will have an opportunity to attend one; not in the foreseeable future, anyway.

This book was written for people like Dave. In a sense, it packages up a workshop for Bible teachers and delivers it in readily accessible form. You might call it a "teach-your-self-to-teach" clinic. And you can either work through it on your own or use it to guide a group study.

I won't pretend that a book on Bible teaching can duplicate all the advantages of a workshop experience. The experience of guided practice and the impact of interpersonal encounters with like-minded people just can't be captured in print. On the other hand, a book like this has its own unique advantages. For one thing, you can go through it as rapidly or as slowly as you wish. And you can go back and review anything that you might have missed the first time around. But the biggest advantage of a workshop-in-a-book is that it's not bound to any particular time or place. You don't have to take a week of vacation time and drive to a conference center to take advantage of it. It's there waiting for you whenever you have the time or inclination to pick it up.

So You've Been Around for a While?

Lest I convey the impression that this book was written only for persons who are new to the task of Bible teaching, let me hasten to say that it will also serve as a good refresher course for those who have been in the business for a while.

There's nothing like a solid review of fundamentals to sharpen a person's skills. When I played high school football, three decades and several pounds ago, we always knew what the agenda was going to be when time came for spring training. It was back to the basics—blocking, tackling, running, kicking. I already knew how to block and tackle. But, every year, the coach insisted that I needed to become reacquainted with those fundamental skills. And he was right, of course.

Even in less hazardous occupations, like seminary teaching—well, less hazardous in some ways—I have come to appreciate the value of reviewing basics. Just a year ago, for example, I sat with an audience of college and university professors and listened to a lecture on the subject, "How to Give a Lecture." How to give a lecture? I had been doing that for twelve years! But I would have been much the poorer for it had I missed that lecture.

In fact, you'll discover that this book doesn't limit itself to blocking and tackling. As valuable as fundamentals are, they can be pursued to a fault, sometimes. I'm thinking about the many times I have heard church teachers complain about annual Bible-teaching clinics, grumbling, "It's the same old stuff every year." While it's true that some of the old stuff is covered in this book, you can be confident that you will pick up a pocketful of new ideas along the way.

Just So We'll Understand Each Other

I have told you why this book was written. I would also like for you to know some of the basic convictions which shaped it. Knowing my presuppositions will help you to understand the approach taken in the pages to follow:

1. Christian teaching is a divine calling.

The Christian teaching ministry, taken in its totality, is a vast enterprise involving thousands of churches and institutions and literally millions of learners. Because of its magnitude, it must depend heavily upon the services of everyday disciples like you and me. There are those who contend that teaching in the church should be placed in the hands of professional superteachers whose superior knowledge and expertise would assure uniformly high quality in religious education. And they can put forward some impressive arguments in favor of this proposal. There's only one problem. It won't work. It's statistically and economically impossible. There just aren't enough superteachers to go around, and even if there were, churches couldn't afford them. And that's why God continues to call people like us to this significant task of Bible teaching. "And God has appointed in the church . . . teachers" (1 Cor. 12:28, RSV).

2. God-called teachers need training.

A sense of calling is no substitute for competence. Paul's advice to Timothy could very well serve as a motto for all Christian teachers: "Do your best to win full approval in God's sight, as a worker who is not ashamed of his work, one who correctly teaches the message of God's truth" (2 Tim. 2:15, TEV).

This verse has three important implications: First, "winning approval in God's sight" requires effort; it means "doing your best." Second, there's a hint that workers who aren't doing their best ought to be ashamed. Third, if teachers have to work hard to teach the message of God's truth correctly, those who approach it casually are likely to end up teaching it incorrectly.

Show me a teacher who feels no need for improvement, and I'll show you a teacher who isn't taking Paul's advice seriously.

3. Teaching skills are improved through practice.

The old saying, "we learn by doing," has a lot of truth in it. No one learns to drive an automobile by merely listening to the instructor. A person learns to drive by grasping the steering wheel, working the brake and accelerator, and handling the shift lever. And children don't learn arithmetic just by reading rules; they work through endless pages of practice problems. Teaching skills are learned "by doing," too.

This principle is demonstrated by the many practical exercises which I have included along with explanations of the teaching process. You will be tempted to skip over them at times. But if you will carry them out faithfully, they will help you sharpen your teaching skills.

4. There is no substitute for basic training in the craft of teaching.

This point relates to a personal bias of mine which is not shared by everybody in religious education today. So much is said nowadays about variations in teaching method—creative expression, role play, simulations, experiential learning, relational Bible study, and the like. I certainly am not opposed to experimentation and innovation in teaching. (For example, I teach a whole course in educational games and simulations.) But I am convinced that we should master the basic tools of teaching before we experiment with the more innovative approaches.

We must walk before we can run. A pianist must master fundamental scales before improvising. The art student needs to acquire a good foundation in basics—balance, light and shadow, color harmony—before developing a unique style. And teachers must gain a solid understanding of the rudiments of their craft before they can use more innovative methods successfully.

This book, therefore, takes a "cornbread and buttermilk" approach to the basics of Bible teaching. (Where I grew up, that means just plain everyday food, not things like crepes suzette or eggs Benedict.) We will touch upon innovative approaches to teaching along the way, but only after establishing a foundation of down-to-earth principles.

5. The Bible is central to Christian teaching.

As you have gathered by now, this book is about Bible teaching. Religious education embraces many other kinds of subject matter—Christian ethics, systematic doctrine, church history, missions, and Christian family living, for example. And obviously, the principles of teaching presented in this book will apply to all of these. But all of it is rooted in the Bible. The Bible contains the primary documents of our faith. What we know about the person and teachings of the Lord Jesus Christ we know because this has been communicated to us through the Scriptures. We appropriate knowledge of God through general revelation and through personal faith. But the Bible teaches us how to interpret that knowledge. The Spirit guides us into all truth, but this guidance is consistently in harmony with biblical revelation.

These observations will explain why this book focuses on Bible teaching. As you move along through subsequent chapters, it will become evident to you that "Bible teaching" is broadly conceived. It means more, much more, than a verse-by-verse explanation of the biblical text. Learning the words of the Bible is not necessarily to be equated with the whole of Bible learning. The words of Scripture become the living word only when they interact dynamically with human experience. More about that later.

6. Bible teaching is a combination of knowing, being, and doing.

Most of us recognize how important it is for a teacher to have a good grasp of subject matter. But there's more to teaching than that. Even an expert in subject matter can bore students to death. Who a teacher is and what she does in class are fully as important as what she knows. This is especially true of Bible teaching, in which the personal dimension takes on such great significance. In Bible study, the teacher's enthusiasm for the task, warmth of relationship with learners, and sensitivity to personal needs becomes as important as expertise in subject matter and skill in educational method.

The teacher's attitude toward the task of teaching will have a lot to do with the climate of Bible study sessions. And that is why this book begins by exploring some basic concepts of teaching, rather than plunging immediately into such things as the nitty-gritty of lesson preparation.

Ready . . . Get Set . . .

As you read the pages to follow, it will occur to you that I have been influenced by yet other biases and presuppositions. But those have to do mostly with the act of teaching, so I'll save them until later on. What you have read already probably has told you enough about the shape of my thinking and the direction of the book to help you decide whether or not you want to turn to chapter 1 and plunge in. I sincerely hope that you will decide in favor of plunging in.

1
What Is Bible Teaching?

One day I reached into my mailbox and pulled out a letter from a man who was trying to publish a book under the title, *Best Sunday School Lessons.* He wanted me to "contribute a lesson" to his book. I turned him down. I had to; because, to me, a Sunday School lesson isn't something you can write down on paper or lock into print. Bible study is the creation of teachers and learners together. To print a lesson in a book would be something like writing down a telephone conversation before it happens.

But that's the way some people think of teaching. They see it as an activity in which a person-who-knows transmits a body of information to persons-who-don't-know in the hope that some of the information will stick in the minds of the latter. Teachers who hold this view like to think in terms of "presenting the lesson."

Lessons aren't made just to be presented. They should be struggled with, tugged at, pulled apart and put back together, mulled over, and grasped at by learners interacting with teachers as both interact with other resources.

A better definition of teaching would be this: "Teaching is helping others to learn." Helping others to learn is quite different from "imparting information" or "presenting the lesson" or "transmitting knowledge."

Have you ever tried to help a small child learn how to tie shoelaces? Just imagine standing over the child and "imparting knowledge" or "presenting a lesson" on shoelace tying. That would be ludicrous. You can't go about it that

15

way. Instead, you must depend upon patient explanations interspersed with repeated demonstrations. Then you say, "Now let's see you try it." As the little one makes the attempt, you offer encouragement and guidance. That is a picture of "helping others to learn."

Learning: the Other Side of Teaching

Notice that this definition of teaching ("helping others to learn") places emphasis on what the learner does, not just on what the teacher says. Teaching and learning are inseparably related.

One of the great teachers of ancient days was the Greek philosopher Socrates. Even though he possessed an impressive amount of knowledge, he refused to teach his students by merely telling them what he knew. He insisted that they discover knowledge for themselves. He helped make such discoveries possible by asking questions that finally led his students to the proper conclusions. Thus, the knowledge that they acquired was actually the product of their own thinking.

This teaching method was known as the maieutic method. The word *maieutic* came from a Greek verb which meant "to serve as a midwife." Just as a midwife helps a mother bring forth a child, the purpose of Socrates the teacher was to bring forth ideas out of the minds of his students.

It is a beautiful concept. And it does so much to explain the relationship of teaching and learning. A midwife might be very knowledgeable and skilled, but she obviously can't do her work alone. A baby's birth is a cooperative effort between mother and midwife. The midwife's role is a helping role. Her job is to make things easier for the mother and child. But the mother must do the actual work of childbearing. The midwife can't do that for her.

Apply this concept to teaching and learning. The teacher has the helping role. She is there to make learning easier for the learner. But the learner himself must do the actual work of learning. The teacher can't do that for him.

The following exercise will help to illustrate the point. You will need a partner for this activity. Your husband or wife, secretary, or one of the children will do nicely. If none of these is available, grab the first friend who happens by.

TEACHING LAB ACTIVITY NO. 1

Make a copy of the following puzzle. (Trace it or run it through a copy machine. Then cut the figure apart on the dotted lines. *Don't let your partner see the puzzle yet.*

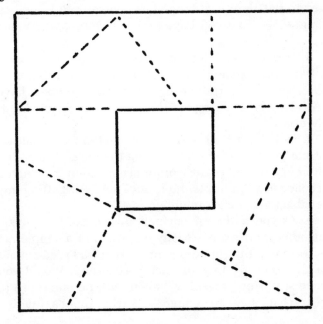

Next, sit back-to-back with your partner. Your partner should have a table in front of him. Give your partner an envelope containing the pieces of puzzle. Place a copy of the complete figure in front of you, but don't let your partner see it. Without turning around, tell your partner how to put the puzzle together. Don't look at what he is doing, and don't touch any of the pieces of the puzzle. Just sit there and "impart" information.

After your partner has either assembled the puzzle or given up, show him the original figure. Then reflect on this experience as you think about the following questions:

1. Did you feel an urge to get your hands on the puzzle your partner was working?

2. Do you agree that it would have been much easier just to put the puzzle together yourself? But had you done this, could you have said that your partner had actually *learned* how to do it?

3. If a teacher "puts together" an interpretation of a Bible passage and merely *tells* her interpretation to the class, can it truly be said that class members have *learned* how to interpret the passage of Scripture for themselves?

4. With your back turned, you couldn't see whether or not your partner was "getting the idea." But is that situation any different from a class session in which a teacher just "presents the lesson" without getting any feedback from class members?

5. As you told your partner how to put the puzzle together, you were actually engaging in a simple act of teaching. But suppose your partner had sneaked out of the room while your back was turned. Would you have still been "teaching," even with no one there to hear what you were saying? Well, what about a situation

in which learners "sneak out of the room" mentally by daydreaming or letting their minds wander?

6. Which is easier; helping a person put together his own interpretation of the Bible, or simply telling him your own interpretation? Which requires more skill, "presenting the lesson" in a prepackaged way, or guiding learners as they discover truth for themselves?

Teaching As Guiding

Picture a stranger wandering into a city which he has never visited before. Given enough time, he might eventually learn something about the city's layout through sheer random effort. But if a local resident comes along and offers guidance, this will greatly increase the probability that the stranger will learn something about the layout of the city. Right?

The same holds true for any other kind of learning situation. Bible study, for instance. A person can wander around in the pages of the Bible without guidance and, given enough time, pick up some biblical information of one kind or another. But give that same person the guidance of a good teacher and the probability that he will gain significant Bible knowledge will be greatly increased.

That's the way the best of teaching operates, where the teacher functions as a guide; pointing the way, setting the learner on the right path, letting him know when he makes a wrong turn, pointing out important landmarks, and making the learner feel good about arriving at the desired destination.

To pursue this line of thinking a little bit further, consider what a guide does *not* do. A guide does not say to the stranger, "I know all about this city and you know nothing about it; so you just stay here and I'll go for you." How much do you suppose the stranger would learn about the city under those circumstances? Nor does the guide say, "You just close your eyes and relax, and I'll tell you when we've arrived at our destination." That would be OK if the stranger had no interest in finding his way around the city again but it wouldn't be a very good way for him to learn something about the city.

You can see what I'm trying to say, of course. A teacher does *not* say, "Look, I know all about the Bible and you know very little; so just let me do all the studying and learning, and I'll tell you what I know when we get together for Bible study."

To further clarify the guiding function of a teacher, let me ask you to work through another teaching lab activity. This one will be simple, not requiring a partner. You'll just need to muster up some imagination.

TEACHING LAB ACTIVITY NO. 2

Let's take a mental excursion. Think your way into the following situation:

You and your four-year-old daughter are present at a community Easter egg hunt in a large city park. Hundreds of eggs have been hidden. An unruly mob of children, most of them older and larger than your little girl, are milling about, waiting impatiently for the starting signal. Your small daughter, shy and inexperienced at this sort of thing, just stands there with a bewildered look on her face.

Suddenly the egg hunt begins! The older kids surge forward grabbing Easter eggs right and left. But your little girl doesn't know where to look. She just wanders around aimlessly, her little basket empty.

Being the veteran Easter egg hunter yourself, you spot a dozen likely hiding places. In fact, you even notice splotches of pink and yellow peeking through one or two clumps of grass.

Your daughter now turns her face toward you and melts your heart with a pathetic look of sheer disappointment. She is on the verge of tears.

What are you going to do?

You might rush over to those hiding places you've spotted, gather up some eggs, and plunk them into your little girl's basket. But wait, wouldn't that take all the fun out of it for her? Wouldn't that rob her of the excitement of finding her own eggs? The better way would be to point her in the right direction, with just enough guidance to help her make the discovery herself.

With this situation in mind, consider these questions:

1. Could a small child eventually find an Easter egg without help? Would her chances be increased by guidance from someone older and more experienced?

2. Is it possible for persons to learn from the Bible without help? If so, why are teachers needed? Is the probability of Bible learning increased by guidance from a teacher?

3. Which is more exciting, to find Easter eggs for yourself, or to watch a grown-up find them for you? Is it more interesting to discover biblical truth for yourself, or to listen to a teacher tell what he has learned?

Teaching As Gardening

Teaching is remarkably like gardening. A gardener is concerned with the growth of plants; a teacher is concerned with the growth of persons.

A gardener knows how to stimulate the potential for growth which lies within the seed; a teacher knows how to bring out the growth potential which lies within the learner.

A gardener gives a great deal of attention to the environment which surrounds his plants, providing ample amounts of sunshine, moisture, and nutrients in the soil. A teacher provides a climate which is conducive to personal growth.

Most importantly, gardeners and teachers alike are "laborers together with God." Any spiritually perceptive gardener will say, "So then neither is he that planteth any thing, neither he that watereth; but God that giveth the increase." For he knows that man cannot *cause* a garden to grow; he can only cooperate with the principles of growth which the Creator has built into the natural order. In similar fashion, a spiritually sensitive Christian teacher will humbly and gladly acknowledge her dependence upon God in the classroom.

God participates in the process of Christian teaching in at least three ways:

First, in his creative work God has endowed human beings with a remarkable capacity for learning. Because this God-given ability operates according to certain principles, Christian teachers are obligated to try to understand how these principles work, just as a gardener must understand certain laws of nature.

Second, in his self-disclosure God has provided a rich resource for Christian learning in the biblical revelation.

Because the Bible is a unique resource of crucial importance, Christian teachers must continually seek to deepen their understanding of it.

Third, in his function as a divine guide, the Spirit of God participates actively in the teaching-learning event—motivating, illuminating, and providing insight. Because the Spirit is actively present in Bible study, teachers and learners alike should clothe their efforts in prayer and in a spirit of dependence upon God.

All three of these points must be kept in proper perspective. To accept one and exclude another is to deny a significant aspect of God's work in Christian teaching. Some people, for example, readily acknowledge the presence of the Holy Spirit in Bible study sessions, but pay little attention to God's design in the dynamics of human learning. While this might at first present a pious impression, it betrays a misunderstanding of—or an indifference to—the way in which the Creator works through orderly processes. Imagine a gardener saying, "It doesn't matter what I plant, or when I plant it, or how I plant it. God will bring the increase, no matter what I do. Any serious gardener would call that a ridiculous attitude. And it has nothing to do with God's ability to grow a garden. That's not the issue. The issue is whether or not the Creator has chosen to work in harmony with his own laws of planting and harvest. And he has.

What is true of gardening is true of teaching, also. A teacher who ignores established principles of learning is like a gardener who plants tomatoes in January snows and expects a harvest in twenty days.

It is possible to make the same error in reverse, of course. A teacher can become so infatuated with slick applications of learning theory and instructional methodology that he ignores the role of the Holy Spirit in the process of Bible study. Christian teachers must always keep in focus our Lord's reminder, "when he, the Spirit of truth, is come, he will guide you into all truth" (John 16:13).

Teaching As Biblical Interpretation

Biblical understanding is basic to all Christian teaching. Jesus said, "If you continue in my word, you are truly my disciples, and you will know the truth, and the truth will make you free" (John 8:31-32, RSV). And this makes biblical knowledge mandatory for the Christian. For there is no way to continue in his Word unless one knows his Word, and there is no way to know his Word apart from the Bible. Our knowledge of the teachings of Jesus grows out of the Gospels, and the Gospels must be understood in the light of the rest of the Bible. One cannot continue in his Word unless he knows his Word.

Thus, biblical interpretation is an essential component of Christian teaching. Think about what this means. Picture a language interpreter trying to help an audience understand a speaker's meaning. A biblical interpreter's task is similar. He tries to help persons in our day understand the meaning of a message first spoken centuries ago.

But we must not understand this task of biblical interpretation too narrowly. The teaching of the biblical revelation is not restricted to a verse-by-verse explanation of the words of the Bible. Biblical interpretation goes beyond this. It is true that genuine Bible study begins with an honest effort to understand the meaning of the text in its historical setting. But if it stops there, the ultimate purpose of Bible study has not been achieved. The final purpose of Bible study is not to tell people things about God, but to lead them to live under the sovereignty of God; not to tell the story of Jesus, but to lead individuals to experience Jesus and live under his lordship. This means that a Bible teacher's task is not only to explain the thirteenth chapter of 1 Corinthians, that great chapter on Christian love, but also to help people become loving persons. And this can't be accomplished just by commenting on the text.

Jesus himself did not always refer to a written text (though he sometimes did) when he taught biblical truth. He dealt with the danger of covetousness, for example, by telling an unforgettable story of a man who exemplified the truth he was trying to get across (Luke 12:13-21).

There are many different ways to interpret the meaning of the Scriptures to learners. If scriptural truths can be revealed through case studies, role play, or the construction of collages, they are just as biblical as they would be if they were conveyed through an exposition of the text.

However it might be taught, the Bible is the bedrock foundation of salvation and Christian discipleship, the well-spring of Christian knowledge. "Rightly dividing the word of truth" must always be a central concern for the Christian teacher.

Let's Summarize

It should be fairly obvious by now that I have some fairly fixed notions about what Bible teaching is and about what it is not. For example, I hope that I have communicated the impression that Bible teaching is *not*

   . . . presenting lessons
     . . . imparting information
       . . . telling pupils what the teacher knows
         . . . a mere performance by a teacher

I have also said some things about what teaching *is*. The important thing, though, is not so much what I think I've said, but what you think you have heard me say. The following teaching lab activity will help you reflect on that:

TEACHING LAB ACTIVITY NO. 3

In the spaces below, jot down at least three ideas about teaching which have come from your reading thus far:

1. _____

_____

_____

2. _____

_____

_____

3. _____

_____

_____

Now, compare what you have written with my own version of what I think I have said in the foregoing pages. All that has been said about teaching thus far can be reduced to three main ideas. Here they are:

• *Teaching and learning are inseparably related.* There is no way to define teaching adequately without reference to learning. A carpenter's work results in a structure of some kind. A cook's work results in food on the table. A teacher's work ought to result in learning.

• *No teacher can transmit learning.* A teacher presents information, provides guidance, offers encouragement, shares resources, and makes explanations. But none of these actions will guarantee that learning will happen. A learner must do his own learning, just as a seed must do its own growing. The teacher's task is to arrange conditions in which learning is most likely to happen.

• *Teachers are co-laborers with God.* God himself participates actively in the teaching-learning process. When God created human beings he gave them the ability to learn. He has provided the Bible, our primary source book for understanding the Christian faith. And the Spirit of God is always present to "guide us into all truth" in Bible study experiences.

2
What Does a Teacher Do?

Our friend Joyce bounced into the office the other day and announced ceremoniously, "You are looking at the new teacher of the young adult class at my church!" Everyone tried to look appropriately impressed. "There's just one thing," she added, just a little more soberly. "What are teachers supposed to do?"

How do you answer that question? You might say, knowingly, "Teachers are supposed to teach." But that's somewhat circular, isn't it? The definition of teaching introduced in the previous chapter suggested that the function of a teacher is to help people learn. But that's also a broad statement. What, exactly, is a teacher supposed to do?

Well, let's start by listing three important functions of a teacher:

First, a teacher builds a learning climate.

Second, a teacher plans and prepares for learning activities.

Third, a teacher leads class sessions.

Even these statements are a bit broad. But we'll break them down into specifics as we go along.

Building a Learning Climate

Have you thought about how much of our behavior is influenced by our surroundings? The atmosphere of a restaurant is such an important ingredient in a pleasurable dining experience that we often are willing to pay a little extra for it. There's something about a funeral home that causes us to lower our voices and maintain a solemn mood. A reverent organ prelude in a quiet sanctuary says, "This is the time and place for worship." A football stadium where bands are playing and fans are shouting says, "This is the time for excitement!" The aroma of good food and the glow of soft candlelight in an elegant diningroom say, "Get ready for an enjoyable meal." In much the same way, the setting for Bible study on Sunday morning should say to all who enter, "This is going to be a good learning experience." That's what it means to "build a learning climate."

A good climate for learning is a composite of several things. The physical setting is one important element. A room decorated in warm colors and equipped with chalkboard, maps, posters, and other learning aids says to everyone present, "This is where learning happens!" The chair arrangement has a lot to do with the learning climate in a class. Chairs in straight rows facing a lectern make it plain that the class members are to be mainly spectators. But chairs placed in a small circle are an open invitation to involvement. Even less noticeable things—room temperature, lighting, and ventilation, for instance—have a great deal to do with the quality of learning experiences.

Ready for some more lab work? Let's apply what has just been said to your own Bible study setting. (If you are not currently teaching, apply the questions in the following exercise to the place where you most often participate in Bible study.)

TEACHING LAB ACTIVITY NO. 4

Use the following questions as a checklist to size up the physical environment in your own Bible study situation.

1. Close your eyes and let your mind take you into

the room where you lead (or participate in) Bible study sessions. Then decide which of the following words most accurately describe your impressions of that room. (Circle one or more words.)

warm   drab   stimulating   cold   sterile   dull
happy   uncomfortable   impressive   dark
interesting   boring   bright   neutral   comfortable
traditional   monotonous   bright

What specific changes would make this room more conducive to learning?

_____ Repaint the walls   _____ Clean up the room
_____ Hang curtains   _____ Hang pictures
_____ Rearrange furni-   _____ Display posters
ture
_____ Improve the light-   _____ Install larger chalk-
ing   board
_____ Provide Maps
_____ Improve ventila-   _____ Install new floor
tion   covering
_____ Adjustment tem-
perature

Another important element in the learning situation is the interpersonal climate. No newcomer to a Bible class should ever fail to receive a warm and genuinely friendly greeting. (For that matter, it doesn't hurt anything to treat regular members this way, too.) Every person in a study group needs to feel that he or she belongs. A person who feels that he is just another digit on the attendance record isn't likely to contribute much energy to the learning task. Like a television viewer, he feels that the program will go on even if he tunes out.

Building a good interpersonal climate in a Bible class calls for more than dutiful handshaking. We all have important personal needs that have a lot to do with our ability to participate happily and effectively in learning groups. We need to be valued by others, to make contributions which are appreciated by others, to be known on a personal basis. We need to be listened to, and be understood; we need to be accepted. As a teacher, you can meet these needs in a variety of subtle ways. Do you listen carefully when a class member expresses an idea? Do you maintain eye-contact or look down at your notes? Do you take questions seriously, or do you treat them as interruptions? As insignificant as these things might seem, they make a difference in the overall climate of your class.

"What makes you feel badly or discourages your attempts to participate in learning groups?" When men and women in adult education classes are asked this question, here are some of the things they say:

"It discourages me when

• I say something in class and the teacher doesn't even look at me.

• I ask a question and no one responds.

• the teacher does all the talking and I don't have a chance to say things that are important to me.

• the teacher interrupts what I am saying.

• only one or two class members seem to have the teacher's ear.

• I do my homework carefully but am given no chance to contribute to the discussion in class.

• no one ever talks with me before or after class unless I start the conversation.

• no one seems to remember my name."

It would be fair to say that a teacher can't maintain a

warm interpersonal atmosphere single-handedly. Every person in a classroom influences the learning climate, for better or worse. Yet, it's up to the teacher to set the pace. We can't say for sure that an open, caring attitude on the part of the teacher will invariably shape the attitudes of class members toward one another; but we can be virtually certain that the interpersonal climate will suffer if the teacher doesn't establish a good pattern.

TEACHING LAB ACTIVITY NO. 5

Use the following questions to assess some of the factors which contribute to, or detract from, good interpersonal climate in your Bible class. If you are uncertain about some of the questions, make a calculated guess:

1. Do you know the name of each class member?
2. Does every member of your class know every other member by name?
3. Are visitors and newcomers *always* introduced by name?
4. Do you establish and maintain eye contact when a class member speaks during the lesson?
5. Do you always attempt, in some way, to help class members feel good about having made a contribution to the discussion?
6. Circle the words below which are most descriptive of the interpersonal climate in your class:

aloof	accepting	casual	congenial
warm	threatening	distant	impersonal
caring	exciting	formal	friendly
stiff	indifferent	so-so	clannish

7. Listed below are a number of suggested actions which have tended to improve interpersonal climate in numbers of Bible classes. Check the ones which you

feel could be implemented successfully in your own class:

_____ Provide name tags at every session

_____ Address members by name when responding to their questions or comments during the lesson

_____ Delegate responsibility for hosting (not just "greeting") visitors and new members

_____ Devise a system that will assure that class members will meet other members socially at least once a month

_____ Assign prayer partners within class membership

_____ Discuss with the class the importance of careful listening and encouraging one another to participate in class discussions

_____ Ask class members to evaluate (orally or in writing) the teacher's influence on their participation in lessons

---

Planning and Preparing for Learning Activities

For a long time I have been impressed by my wife's ability to entertain people in our home with such skill and composure. I never cease to be amazed at the fact that she can come home from a busy day at her office and, in two hours or less, have a delicious hot dinner ready for sixteen guests with a minimum of frustration and bother. I'm observant enough to know that it doesn't just happen. It all begins when, well in advance of the occasion, she makes out a menu and posts it on the refrigerator door for easy reference. She uses that menu as a guide for preparing a shopping list. Most of the components of the meal are prepared in advance. When the time comes to put it all together, the ingredients

for the tossed salad are waiting, cool and crisp, in the refrigerator; the roast is ready to take out of the slow cooker; and
rolls are ready to pop into the oven. Even the table has
been set in advance. (One of the keys to her success is, of
course, my services as first assistant chef.)

No, I'm not off the subject. For those who have eyes to
see and ears to hear, we have an important lesson here in
the art of successful Bible teaching. A good Bible study session doesn't just happen, any more than one of those dinner
parties does. It's the product of careful planning and advance
preparation. Like an expert cook, a teacher must plan the
menu (decide what is to be taught in the session), collect
the necessary ingredients (gather teaching materials), prepare components in advance (study guides, lecture outlines,
posters, case studies, and so forth), and set the table for study
(prepare the room and equipment).

Deciding what is to be taught. When you think about it,
goal-setting is an important first step in all kinds of worthwhile endeavors. You begin planning a motor trip by deciding on a destination. You start a new house by drawing plans.
Your highway department lays out a route before building
a new road. We begin our spring gardening every year by
deciding what we want to plant. A sculptor doesn't put chisel
to marble before he envisions what he wants to end up with.
So it is with teaching. The logical starting place is the setting
of goals for teaching and learning. It isn't enough for a Bible
study session to be just good; it should be good *for something.*

Ideally, class members ought to help set learning goals.
(More about this in chapter 5.) But, in actual practice, goals
for study sessions are usually born in the head of the teacher.
Remember how teaching was compared to the work of a
guide in the previous chapter? A guide often says something
like, "No, we don't want to take that street; let's take this

one." When a teacher sits down to prepare a lesson and decides on a particular teaching-learning goal, she is saying, in effect, "We'll go in this direction with this lesson, and not that one." The selection of goals is part of a teacher's guidance function.

Let's look at an illustration of that point. Suppose you develop an interest in painting with oils, and you go to an art teacher for lessons. She probably would say, "Fine. But before you paint, you must learn to draw. You must master basics, such as simple line drawing, shading, formal and informal balance, perspective, and texture. Then you must learn something about color harmony, the blending of colors, and brush technique. Then you will be ready to do oil painting." What is really happening in such a situation? The teacher is pointing to certain learning goals which ought to be pursued. And this, in itself, is a part of teaching.

Breaking a major goal (becoming an oil painter) down into a series of subgoals (learning about balance, perspective, and color harmony) is basic to any ambitious learning task— playing tennis, flying an airplane, programming computers, or speaking a foreign language. But sometimes we don't think of Bible study in this way. It never occurs to some people that Bible study ought to be broken down into specific learning tasks, all pointing toward some major goal. Ask them what their purpose is for any given class meeting, and they will answer with the generality: "To study the Bible."

An art student doesn't just "study art" without ever thinking of more definite goals. The goal this week might be to achieve a proper sense of balance in freehand sketches. Next week he might try to learn various shading techniques. After that he might try to learn something about perspective. Such goals are tangible and manageable. They lend substance and meaning to "studying art."

Apply the same principle to Bible study. Let's say that members of a Bible study group want to learn more about the book of Revelation. They agree on that broad goal, but they don't quite know where to "take hold." They need someone to help them identify tangible learning goals, goals that will move them toward an increased understanding of Revelation. And that's where a teacher comes in. In the first session, for instance, a teacher might suggest that the students need to learn something about the characteristics of apocalyptic literature in order to comprehend the nature of the book of Revelation. There's a good chance that some of the students, being unfamiliar even with the term, "apocalyptic," would never have chosen this learning goal for themselves. But the teacher, functioning as a guide, says, "Let's take this road first."

Setting teaching-learning goals for a lesson requires something more than specifying a portion of Scripture to be studied. So much can be learned from the study of a single Bible passage, in many instances, that it's hard to know what to include and what to leave out. Take the Beatitudes of Jesus in Matthew 5:3-12, for instance; just ten short verses. Learning the meaning of the key terms in verse 3 alone— "blessed," "poor in spirit," "kingdom of heaven"—could easily fill the time available in a single Bible study period. And learning the biblical meaning of the terminology in all the Beatitudes would be but a first step in interpreting them. The question of each Beatitude's meaning for today's believers would yet remain. This brief passage could keep a Bible class busy for a month or more. How do you manage to deal with it in a single, one-hour session? This is one of the questions which must be answered as the teacher sets lesson goals.

Planning learning activities. The first step in planning a journey is deciding on a destination. The second step is planning how to get there. Preparation for teaching sessions is like that. The first step is to decide where you want to go with the lesson; then you decide what kinds of learning activities will get you there.

At the risk of sounding like a nit-picker, I want to remind you that a teacher can't "transfer" any kind of knowledge to a learner. "I can't learn them kids anything!" might be terrible English, but it contains a kernel of educational truth. Indeed, a teacher can't "learn" anybody. Every individual must learn for himself.

What a teacher can do is to arrange for the learners to have experiences which might lead to learning. All learning results from experience. This is true of accidental learning as well as of planned learning. A small child reaches for the handle of a pan of boiling water on the stove and is painfully burned, for example. As a result of this *experience,* a lesson about pans of boiling water is indelibly imprinted in his mind. He has learned. A nine-year-old girl is given a list of books of the Bible and is asked to repeat them over and over again. As a result of this *experience,* she learns to recite the books of the Bible. She has learned. A man on the street buys a "bargain" watch from a peddler, and it turns out to be junk. He says, "I surely did learn a lesson." And he did, as a result of an *experience.*

The teacher's job in developing a lesson plan is not so much to arrange the subject matter in a neat outline; but, rather, to arrange for the learners to have *experiences* which will result in learning. A lesson plan is not an outline of the subject matter to be covered. It is a description of study activities which will lead learners to interact with the lesson material so as to learn from those experiences.

The special teaching skill required for this kind of planning is the ability to make the learning activity fit the learning goals for a given lesson. Unfortunately, some teachers never vary their approach in a Bible-study session. Invariably, they (a) have class members read the Bible passage, one verse to a customer, (b) make various comments on the Bible passage, reading selected (underlined) quotations from the teacher's quarterly, (c) urge the class to go out and do whatever the lesson was about, and (d) call on someone to close the class session with prayer.

"What is the worst teaching method?" someone once asked Gaines S. Dobbins. "The one that is used all the time," the wise teacher replied. And he was right. Can you imagine a mechanic who uses only one wrench, or a surgeon who uses but one instrument, or a football quarterback who knows only one play?

There are many ways to learn. We can learn some things by listening to someone talk. But we can't learn everything that way. Would you be willing to trust yourself to an automobile driver who had learned to drive only by listening to a series of lectures on the subject? Would you employ a typist who had never touched a typewriter, but had only sat in a classroom and listened to a teacher give instructions? And what about a dentist who had never practiced with a drill? The point is, some things must be learned through direct experience.

Other things may be learned through secondhand experience. For example, we may learn something about the horrors of starvation through the stark realism of a documentary film on world hunger. Or we may learn more about the meaning of faith by reading and discussing a book about the life of a person who has walked with God through distressing experiences.

Some kinds of learning may best be accomplished through practice and drill. If you want to learn the vocabulary of a foreign language, there is no substitute for memorization and repeated usage of the words. The printed page is a good medium for learning facts and dates associated with biblical history; but a motion picture film designed for that purpose would be a waste of money, since the same result can be achieved through cheaper methods.

The teacher's task in lesson planning is to master the material well enough to know what should be accomplished through the study of that material, then to make a wise selection of learning activities, much as a golfer chooses just the right club for each stroke.

(More on this subject in chapter 6, where we'll go into greater detail on the subject, "How to Develop a Plan for Teaching a Lesson.")

The following teaching lab activity should give you a greater appreciation for the point made earlier—that we do our learning through a variety of experiences. And it should demonstrate, by implication at least, the fact that learning must be achieved through different kinds of teaching methods.

TEACHING LAB ACTIVITY NO. 6

Instructions: Below you will see a list of fairly common learning experiences. Look through the list and (1) place a check mark in front of each thing that you have learned at one time or another, then (2) in the space to the right of each of these items, jot down a word or a phrase indicating *how* you learned it.

As an example, here's how I would describe one of my early learning experiences:

_____ Live electric current is dangerous.	Stuck hairpins into wall outlets
WHAT I LEARNED	HOW I LEARNED IT
_____ multiplication tables	_____
_____ writing in longhand	_____
_____ riding a bicycle	_____
_____ disliking some foods	_____
_____ sewing	_____
_____ disliking some people	_____
_____ praying	_____
_____ using a telephone directory	_____
_____ cooking	_____
_____ religious doctrines	_____
_____ valuing money	_____
_____ driving a car	_____
_____ using the alphabet	_____

Take another look at the teaching lab activity. Notice the different kinds of learning illustrated there. Things like learning multiplication tables and the alphabet require mental effort. Educational psychologists call this "cognitive" learning. Learning to "like," "dislike," or "value" things has to do with emotions, "gut feelings," attitudes. This is called "affective" learning. (That will make more sense when you think about what we mean by the word *affection,* which is closely related to the word *affective.* They both have to do with feelings.) Writing in longhand, riding a bicycle, and driving a car call for a combination of mental and physical skills. The term "psychomotor" is often used to label such learning. ("Psycho" refers, of course, to our psychological makeup, and "motor" refers to bodily movement.)

I don't want to leave the impression that all learning experiences can be classified neatly as "cognitive," "affective," or "psychomotor," because a great many of the things we learn involve two, or even all three, of these categories. Driving a car, for instance, certainly calls for cognitive learning (knowing facts) as well as psychomotor learning (using the steering wheel). But, on the other hand, we can say that most learning experiences lie *primarily* within one of these three categories. Using a telephone directory calls mainly for cognitive learning, although a bit of psychomotor skill is involved.

You might be wondering at this point what all of this has to do with "planning learning activities," which, as you might recall, is the subject we're supposed to be thinking about at the moment. The answer to that question will become clearer in chapters 5 and 6. But for the time being, let me explain that certain approaches to teaching seem to achieve cognitive learning better than other approaches;

and some are better suited for affective learning. The same holds true for learning in the psychomotor category, of course. Using these labels—cognitive, affective, psychomotor—helps us to match up teaching goals and learning activities. For example, if we want to change certain attitudes through the study of a portion of Scripture, and we consciously classify this as an affective aim, this will lead us quite naturally to consider methods which are usually associated with affective learning. In other words, classifying our teaching goals will help us to think about them in relationship to teaching-learning activities.

Preparing for learning activities. We went to a large fireworks display the other night. The thing that impressed me was the massive amount of preparation that must have gone into it. The show, which actually lasted only twenty minutes or so, was a real spectacular. It went off with clockwork precision. But that was possible only because someone had worked all day—probably longer—to set it up right.

"Set it up right." Not a bad slogan for the Bible teacher. Good preparation is the key to smoothly operating study sessions. A fellow in the television business once told me that fifty-six hours of work goes into the filming of an average thirty-second commercial. I'm not suggesting that the ratio has to be that high, but I am convinced that what happens in a Bible study session is largely determined by what the teacher does before the class assembles.

What needs to be done, exactly? Well, for one thing, like the hostess who prepares and refrigerates all the ingredients for her tossed salad in advance, the teacher needs to assemble study materials. If a case study is to be used, copies will need to be prepared for class members. If the teacher plans to lecture, he might prepare an outline of the main points on a sheet of poster board. If a resource person is to be brought into class, arrangements will have to be made in advance. If the lesson plan calls for small-group discussion, a written discussion guide will be needed for each group.

Then, of course, the teacher needs to "set the table," arranging chairs and tables, setting up interest centers, providing extra pencils and sheets of paper, checking on the supply of chalk, erasers, felt-tip markers, and so on. If possible, the teacher ought to enlist class members to help with these tasks. But with help or without it a teacher ought to accept personal responsibility for having everything ready to go when the class comes together.

Leading Class Sessions

"What are teachers supposed to do?" Thus far we've focused on two answers to that question: (1) Teachers are supposed to build a learning climate; (2) Teachers are supposed to plan and prepare for learning activities. Now we come to a third (and probably the most visible) function of teachers, leading class sessions.

When you lead the class in Bible study sessions, always keep three major purposes in mind: First, help the learners want to learn. Second, guide them in learning activities. Third, help them to know when they have learned. The first of these functions we call "motivating"; the second, "guiding"; the third, "evaluating."

Motivating learners. I have seen a certain kind of miracle happen on several occasions. Picture a group of persons sitting in a room, idling their mental motors. They aren't interested in anything in particular. Just chattering. Then an enthusiastic teacher enters the room and, within a few minutes, the group is alive with learning activity—pondering a problem, asking questions, hurling comments across the room, arguing a point here and there, searching for information—

in all of it, propelled by the excitement generated by the teacher. That's a picture of motivation for learning.

But where does it come from? How do you manufacture it? Motivation is easy to recognize, but hard to produce. That's why participants in Bible teaching conferences so often ask, "How can I get class members to take part in the lesson?"

To be honest, the art of motivating learners is a complicated process. It isn't something you learn to do in three easy steps. It relates, in part, to the personality of the teacher. But don't be misled. You don't have to bounce into class grinning like JoJo the Clown in order to be an effective motivator. Last summer I attended a professional meeting in a large motel. Next door to our conference room someone was staging a "motivational seminar" for sales personnel. Their meeting room was plastered with slogans like, "Think success!" and "You can do it if you think you can!" Sometimes their cheers and pep songs were so raucous we could hardly hear ourselves think. And outside their room was a giant photograph of the siminar leader, with the title in glittering four-inch letters, "OUR BALL OF FIRE!" Believe me, friend, that definitely is not what I have in mind when I speak of motivating learners.

Sure, it helps to be charming, energetic, and winsome. But genuine human warmth, old-fashioned friendliness, far outweighs those attributes. In my own educational pilgrimage, nothing else has kindled my desire to learn so much as teachers who really cared about what I was doing. And I suspect that you have found it the same way.

Your personal enthusiasm for the lesson material will also have a strong bearing on the motivational level of the persons you teach. If you try to teach without having a lively interest in the lesson yourself, you can't expect class members to generate much enthusiasm for it. Enthusiasm and dullness are both contagious. For twenty-eight years I've remembered what one of my college English professors said when her assignment of yet another term paper was greeted by the usual chorus of groans and cries of anguish. "Now, students," she said sweetly, "you must not tell yourselves, 'I have to write a paper.' You ought to choose a subject, then keep reading on that subject until it kindles your interest, and you can say, 'I have a paper to write!'" And that was excellent advice; not only for English students, but also for Bible class teachers who find themselves saying too frequently, "Oh, my, I've got to teach a lesson again."

One of the most powerful ways to motivate learners is to convince them that the lesson is addressed to them, personally. Too often people study the Bible as though it were an artifact under glass in a museum case; an ancient book about olden people in olden times. Our task as teachers of the Bible is not to make the message relevant. It's already relevant; disturbingly so. Our task is to help twentieth-century people discover that in the ancient text there is a message "living and active, sharper than any two-edged sword, piercing to the division of soul and spirit, of joints and marrow, and discerning the thoughts and intentions of the heart" (Heb. 4:12, RSV).

For example, present-day disciples are prone to contemplate 1 Corinthians 13 in a detached sort of way, speaking adoringly of this "great love chapter." It's easy enough to agree with the apostle Paul that "love is patient and kind; . . . is not arrogant or rude. . . . Does not insist on its own way; . . . is not irritable or resentful," so long as you keep the text at arm's length. But when, in the context of Bible study, we are compelled to use the biblical criteria as a measuring stick for our own lives ("Am *I* patient with my employees?" Do *I* insist on having my own way at home? in the church?" "Am *I* irritable with my teenage children? my parents? my husband or wife?"), the potential for significant learning increases substantially. Bible study of this kind is not always comfortable, but it's not sleep inducing, either.

Psychologist Jerome Bruner, an expert on the theory of teaching, has said that teachers ought to be concerned about three aspects of motivation for learning. The teacher must (1) get "learning behavior" started, (2) keep it going, and (3) channel it in the right direction. By "learning behavior," Bruner means all the kinds of activity that lead to learning, such as pondering questions, discussing ideas, reasoning, or searching for information. People don't always come to class ready to plunge into such activities. You know this from experience. You've seen people come to class with other things on their minds, chatting idly about this or that. One of the responsibilities of the teacher, in every class session, is to come up with some plan for getting class members involved in the learning process.

But Bruner's second point is important, too. For all of us have seen study sessions sag in the middle even after getting off to a good start. As a matter of fact, it's even harder to sustain interest after thirty minutes of study than it is to gain attention at the beginning, simply because most people begin to tire physically and mentally after sitting that long. This is one of the best reasons I know for using more than one kind of learning activity during a class period. An occasional change of pace—shifting from a lecture to a small-group activity—does a lot to sustain interest.

When I think of Bruner's third point, the one about channeling learning behavior in the right direction, I'm reminded of some of the rabbit-chasing I've witnessed in classrooms. There was nothing wrong with the level of interest on these occasions. Students would raise questions, argue, present evidence, and froth and fume for the entire period—but to no useful purpose. When it was over, everyone realized that we had just gone in circles. It isn't enough just to get learners to expend mental energy. A part of the teacher's job is to coax them to expend it for the right reasons. But this is directly related to the task of guiding learning activities, which we will discuss shortly. Before we do that, let me introduce a teaching lab activity that will help you do some more thinking about motivation for learning.

TEACHING LAB ACTIVITY NO. 7

Think back to one of the best learning experiences you've ever had. You found it interesting; perhaps even exciting. You enjoyed it so much that no one had to apply any pressure to make you learn. You learned because you wanted to learn. And what you learned gave you a real sense of satisfaction.

Don't limit yourself to any particular kind of learning experience. It might have been in a formal course; but it might have been in an informal setting. Perhaps you had a teacher; but maybe you learned on your own.

Take a few minutes to recall such a learning experience; then try to answer the following questions about it.
1. What did you learn?
2. How did you learn it?
3. Why did you want to learn it?
4. What kept you interested enough to continue applying yourself to the learning task?

Finally, do some thinking about those questions and your answers to them in relation to your work as a teacher. What can you do to help learners get that much satisfaction out of Bible study experiences?

Guiding learning activities. Recall that meeting between Philip and the high-ranking Ethiopian official somewhere on the road between Jerusalem and Gaza (Acts 8:26 ff.). Philip found the man sitting in his chariot reading from the prophecy of Isaiah, and he asked the man, "Do you understand what you are reading?" The Ethiopian, evidently in doubt about the meaning of the passage, answered, "How can I understand it, unless someone guides me?"

If ever there was a clarion call for Bible teachers, we find one here in the poignant question of that Ethiopian. In a hundred different ways, that same call is being sounded today; by persons who unexpectedly visit your Bible class, by youth who would sooner die than admit to the deep doubts that bedevil their minds, and by those who come to your class regularly and say by their very presence, "How can I understand it, unless someone guides me?"

How does a teacher provide guidance? In numerous ways. Picture a teacher seated within a circle of young adults, drawing them out with carefully formulated questions. See a teaching leader leaning across a table where a handful of youth are working together on a study project. Visualize a class of men pondering the complexities of a case study as their teacher writes their comments on a chalkboard, or a teacher of women distributing a pencil-and-paper questionnaire. These are pictures of teachers guiding learning activities. And these are only a few representative examples from among numerous possibilities chosen to underscore a point made in the first chapter of this book, namely, that leading a class in Bible study is something more than presenting information.

There is no better example of this point than the teaching of Jesus. Gospel accounts provide illuminating descriptions of varied approaches used by the Master Teacher to guide learners in their quest for truth.

He often used questions for this purpose. Have you ever noticed how often he refused to give direct answers to persons who asked him questions? He preferred, instead, to ask counter questions. For example, when certain men asked, "Is it lawful to pay taxes to Caesar, or not?" (Mark 12:14 RSV), he asked to see a coin, then posed the question, "Whose likeness and inscription is this?" (v. 16). A lawyer asked, "Teacher, what shall I do to inherit eternal life?" Jesus countered with the question, "What is written in the law?" (Luke 10:25-26, RSV). And it was not uncommon for the Teacher to end a parable with a penetrating question, such as, "Which of these three, do you think, proved neighbor to the man who fell among the robbers?" (v. 36, RSV).

Parables play a significant role in the teaching of Jesus. They provide an important insight into the teaching method of Jesus. In every instance where Jesus told a parable, he could have simply "imparted" the truth he was seeking to teach. Why didn't he? Instead of going to the trouble to tell a parable, why didn't he simply state whatever principle he wanted to communicate? Instead of relating the story of the good Samaritan, why didn't he just say, "Every man is your neighbor"? Instead of telling a story about a foolish rich man, why didn't he just come out and say, "Anybody who is so obsessed with earthly treasures that he forgets God is a fool"?

Jesus himself gave a theological explanation for his use of parables (Matt 13:10-17). But, in view of his marvelous insight into the workings of the mind, was there not also a psychological reason? A truth stated in the form of a proposition may easily escape the hearers. But a truth buried in a story, one which the hearer must dig out for himself, is much more likely to lodge in the mind.

A great deal more might be said about the teaching methods of Jesus. Whole volumes have been written on the subject. But that isn't our purpose here. The point is that there are many ways to guide learners in their search for knowledge, and that the teaching of Jesus is an excellent illustration of this truth.

We won't start examining specific types of teaching-learning activities just yet. That will come later, in chapters 6 and 8. Instead, let me suggest three rules of thumb to keep in mind when leading a class session. Each of these principles requires the teacher to walk a tightrope between undesirable extremes.

1. Provide positive leadership without dominating the class.

2. Allow adequate time for learning without letting the session drag.

3. Challenge the learners without threatening them.

The first principle relates to the teacher's leadership style. On one extreme there are highly authoritarian teachers, drill-sergeant types, who like to call all the shots. They frown at unscheduled questions from members, discourage all deviant points of view, and stick to the lesson plan more rigidly than the aerospace people follow a prelaunch countdown. On the other extreme are the laissez-faire types who won't lift a finger to give guidance to the class session even when it disintegrates into chaos. They have a maddening habit of sitting there and grinning sweetly while the discussion sways whichever way the wind happens to blow.

A teacher must provide enough guidance to give structure and purpose to the class session. The best tool for doing this is a good lesson plan built around concrete goals. But a lesson plan is just a tool not the end product. The end product of any study session should be learning. If the lesson plan gets in the way of learning, the teacher should be prepared to alter it.

A women's Bible class was studying Matthew 27, which tells of Jesus' trial before Pilate and his crucifixion. Verses 3-10 refer to the death of Judas Iscariot, saying that "he went and hanged himself." When the teacher mentioned the circumstances of Judas' death, a young woman started weeping. As it turned out, this young lady was deeply distressed over the suicidal death of a sister and she was particularly troubled by the erroneous belief that suicide was an "unpardonable sin." For the rest of the session the whole class focused attention on this young woman's needs; and, in the process, they learned things that had not been anticipated by the teacher's lesson plan. Fortunately, the teacher was sensitive enough to recognize an unscheduled "teachable moment."

The second principle has to do with the teacher's use of time in the classroom. And, again, it is important to strike a good balance. On one hand, the session shouldn't drag; that is a certain road to boredom. The teacher should be prepared to rescue the class discussion when it begins to wallow in trivialities. On the other hand, beating the bell to the conclusion of the lesson should not become such an obsession that members are allowed no time to think, talk, or reflect on questions. One of the hardest lessons for teachers to learn is that it takes a few moments to process a thought question before answering it. When you ask a question like, "What does the eleventh chapter of Hosea tell us about the nature of God?" you can't expect the average learner to respond intelligently within five seconds. But many teachers will ask a question like that, pause only long enough to catch a breath, then dash in and answer it themselves. Sooner or later, the people in such classes learn that they are not really expected to think.

Teachers who get itchy about "covering the lesson" before

the period ends communicate their impatience in a variety of ways. Some look at their watches whenever anyone else dares to say something; some fumble with their notes or leaf through their Bibles while others are trying to speak. Some, regarding any comment from a member as an interruption, respond impatiently: "Yes. But as I was saying, so forth and so on."

TEACHING LAB ACTIVITY NO. 8

Students sometimes fail to respond to questions posed by their teachers simply because they aren't given enough time to think it over. Teachers should train themselves to pause after asking questions. How long? Professional educators suggest that thirty seconds is about right. It sounds simple enough. But, as the following lab activity will demonstrate, it really isn't all that easy.

The following procedures are given in three versions. Which one you use depends on how many other people you can get involved in it. Procedure A is best, B is next best, and C is to be used if you can't do either of the other two.

PROCEDURE A: You can use this procedure only if you are actually teaching a Bible class. Include some thought questions in your lesson plan. Make them fairly difficult; don't use questions that can be answered "off the top of the head." Force yourself to pause at least thirty seconds after asking each question. Let someone in the class, enlisted before the session, time your pauses.

PROCEDURE B: You'll need to enlist one or two other persons for this procedure. Sit down with them in a face-to-face arrangement. Say: "I want to ask you to help me with a practice-teaching activity." Then remain absolutely silent for thirty seconds; don't smile, don't look away, don't say anything. Chances are, the silence will be deafening. Then ask this question: "What is the most striking reference to teaching in all the Bible?" Again, pause in silence for a full thirty seconds. (By the way, the question has no definite answer. It was designed *not* to be answered.) Now, before your assistants question your sanity, explain to them that you are experimenting to see what a thirty second pause feels like. Then practice two or three more thirty-second periods of silence with them. The effect will be better if you will look each other straight in the eye during these pauses.

PROCEDURE C: If you can't enlist anyone else to help, do it this way. Ask a question, just any question, aloud. Then pause in silence for a full thirty seconds. (Time yourself with a watch or a clock with a sweep-hand.) Do this two or three times. The purpose of this activity is to get a "feel" for pauses of this length.

The third principle has to do with maintaining just the right amount of tension in learning situations; enough to stimulate learning, but not so much as to threaten learners. As teachers lead study sessions, they should challenge class members to think, to clarify vague ideas, to give reasons for their personal points of view. On the other hand, they should be careful not to embarrass individuals by asking questions which are too difficult for them or pressing them to do things which are beyond their abilities. If learners are not challenged, they will become bored; if they are challenged too vigorously, they will become discouraged.

Let me illustrate what it means to challenge learners. Assume that you are teaching a lesson based on Matthew 5:27-
32, a passage in which Jesus speaks about adultery, lust, and
divorce. You could simply lecture on the passage and its
contemporary meaning while your class members sit in silence, hopefully listening to your views. But suppose you
could get them to wrestle with the meaning of these teachings in relation to life as they know it? Wouldn't that be
more effective?

There is a simple technique which would lend itself to
this purpose. You prepare for it by putting up six hand-let-
tered posters around the room. They have these words on
them: (1) Strongly Disagree, (2) Disagree, (3) Disagree with
Reservations, (4) Agree with Reservations, (5) Agree and (6)
Strongly Agree. Then you read capsule descriptions of hypothetical situations. The class members are asked to indicate their agreement or disagreement with what was done
in each situation by standing near the poster which expresses
their point of view. For example, you might pose this situation: "Harold Bird went with friends to a famous art gallery
while vacationing in Europe. But when he came across several paintings of nudes, he immediately left the gallery, saying that it was lustful to look at such paintings." After class
members have positioned themselves near the posters which
most nearly express their respective attitudes, they should
then be given an opportunity to explain their positions. This
process usually produces interesting differences of opinion.
The important thing, however, is that it challenges learners
to express their viewpoints, testing them out in the give-
and-take of class discussion.

Now let's consider the other side of the coin. While it is
desirable to prod learners into active involvement with the
lesson, you'll want to be careful not to embarrass or intimi-

date them. The procedure described above, for example, might be a bit much for a group of adults who tend to be a little on the stuffy side. When this is the case, you can modify the same procedure by turning it into a pencil-and-paper activity. Just have class members indicate their attitudes toward each situation by jotting them down on paper. This should be much less threatening than having to (of all things!) move out of their chairs.

Leading the study session is probably the most exciting, and certainly the most demanding, part of the teacher's task. In the give-and-take of teaching-learning activities, the teacher is called upon to generate enthusiasm, provide resources, offer information, excite curiosity, give gentle guidance, resolve conflicts, encourage the timid, restrain the domineering, review, summarize, evaluate, and challenge. It doesn't sound easy. And it isn't. But it is possible, through experience and practice, to develop one's proficiency in the art.

Evaluating learning. To have a well-rounded picture of the teacher's task, we need to add one other element. Evaluation. Why bother to shoot at a target if you're not going to check to see whether you hit it? Who would watch the start of a race without paying attention to the finish line? And why invest time and energy into teaching and learning activities if no one is concerned about the result? Evaluation is the process by which you measure the result of everything else you do as a teacher.

But evaluation is important to learners, as well as to teachers. Earlier, I suggested three purposes which teachers ought to keep in mind when they lead learning activities. Remember them? First, help the learners want to learn. Second, guide them in learning activities. Third, help them to know it when they have learned. We're now focusing on that third point. Learners need to be aware of what they have learned, and even what they have failed to learn. Why? There are at least two good reasons. First, evaluation can help channel learning efforts in the right direction. Second, it can provide powerful motivation for learning.

One summer I was leading a demonstration Bible study session for a group of adult Bible teachers. We were exploring the New Testament concept of Christian love, usually called *agape* (ah-GAH-pay). I had become thoroughly engrossed in the subject during my preparation for the session and had surveyed most of the passages in the New Testament where the word is used; and we examined many of these during the session. Toward the end of the period, one of the teachers raised her hand: "I could never lead a session like this one, because I don't know that much about the subject. How does a teacher learn the kinds of things that you have shared with us?"

It was a good question, and I was glad she had asked it; because it gave me a good chance to show how useful a common Bible-study tool could be. "I just used a concordance to locate the Scriptures we looked at today," I explained. Then, sensing that this was not entirely clear to everybody, I asked, "How many of you make regular use of a concordance?" Just a few raised their hands. Then we spent a few minutes talking about the uses of Bible concordances, and I made some impromptu assignments, asking various individuals to look up references on important biblical words like "righteousness," "sin," "repentance," and so forth. I also tried to point out the advantages of larger concordances, the ones that are more complete than the ones we have in our Bibles.

The next day, two or three members of the group came back full of enthusiasm. For the first time, they had come to appreciate the real value of a concordance. Heretofore, they had used concordances only to look up a scriptural quotation here and there. But now they had learned to use a wonderful resource for studying biblical themes.

Two things had happened; both of them related to what I mean by evaluation. First, these individuals had been helped to identify something that they had not previously learned, a weak spot in their equipment as teachers of the Bible. By concentrating on the assignments that I had given them, they worked to correct that deficiency. (This is what I meant earlier when I said, "evaluation can help channel learning efforts in the right direction.") Then the second thing happened. Having learned how to use a concordance in a new way, they found tremendous satisfaction in this achievement. And, of course, I did everything possible to reinforce their sense of accomplishment. (And this illustrates the point that evaluation can "provide powerful motivation for learning.")

You will note, also, that evaluation of learning isn't necessarily tied to formal procedures such as giving tests and issuing report cards. (Not that these would hurt anything in Bible study.) Whatever a teacher does to help class members know that they have learned, or that they need to learn something better, is evaluation. This often happens in subtle ways. I remember, for example, an occasion in a workshop for adult Bible teachers when I started the session by asking, "What are the characteristics of adult learners?" This produces a flurry of well-informed responses. Finally, I stepped back from the chalkboard on which I had been writing their responses and said, quite sincerely; "I can't believe this; you've outlined my whole lecture." I was saying, in effect, "You know this stuff hands down; we don't need to spend more time on this." Really, it was an evaluative comment.

Looking Back

"What does a teacher do?" That's the question with which this chapter began. To answer the question, I suggested that a teacher:

- Builds a Learning Climate
- Plans and Prepares for Learning Activities
- Leads Class Sessions

Learning climate depends partially on physical surroundings but, more importantly, on personal relationships. Every member of a learning group wants to feel valued and accepted. Every person wants to feel that he is making a worthwhile contribution. When members of a Bible class know and care for one another, they communicate more openly and freely. And the teacher's example has a lot to do with establishing these patterns.

Planning and preparing for learning activities is a three-stage process. First, the teacher decides what is to be taught, setting goals for the session. Second, she plans learning activities which are compatible with those goals, remembering that some methods are best suited for factual learning and others for the learning of values and attitudes. Third, the teacher prepares materials, sets up the room, and makes other kinds of advance preparation for the session.

Leading class sessions is the most visible part of a teacher's work. As leader, the teacher motivates learners, guides learning activities, and, in a variety of ways, helps class members evaluate their learning efforts.

Motivation is a threefold process in which the teacher finds ways to get learning activity started, keep it going, and channel it in the right direction.

The art of guiding learning activities is at its best when the teacher can exert positive leadership without dominating the class, provide adequate time for learning without letting the session lag, and challenge the learners without threatening them.

Evaluation has two main purposes—to motivate and to give direction to learning efforts. When one learns something new, the sense of achievement is highly satisfying. A teacher ought to take every opportunity to recognize such achievements. And, by helping class members to discover what they need to learn, or learn better, the teacher can contribute to the productive use of time and effort.

As you can see, this chapter has covered a lot of territory. You might have had trouble absorbing it all. But don't worry about that. The purpose has been to paint a picture of the teacher's work in broad strokes. So, if you got a general impression of the task of teaching, this will suffice for now. Almost everything we've covered in this chapter will be treated in greater detail later on.

3
What Teachers Ought to Know

I really felt that Wade would make a good Bible teacher. He was intelligent, had a pleasing personality, and was highly respected in professional circles and within the church. There was no question about his commitment to Christ. But when I mentioned this to him one day, he replied, "But I don't know enough to teach the Bible." He was being unduly modest, of course, but his remark set me thinking. Just what should a person know in order to be a successful Bible teacher? That's the question I want to tackle in this chapter.

But this poses two difficulties that I'd like to call to your attention at the very beginning. You'll be in a better position to appreciate the first one after working through the next teaching lab activity.

TEACHING LAB ACTIVITY NO. 9

The instructions for this activity are simple. But you'll have to give it some thought. And you will need to enlist the help of five other persons.

Here's what you do:

First, on a sheet of paper, list *ten* answers to the question, "What should a Bible teacher know?" Chances are, you'll run out of ideas after the first five. But keep asking about it, and you'll come up with more.

Second, ask five other people to do the same thing. They, too, will want to stop after jotting down two or three answers. But encourage them to keep at it until they have thought of at least ten.

Third, compile a master list by combining all the answers, yours and the others. Avoid duplicate answers. After an item appears once, don't list it again.

How many answers did you get in all? How many would you have gotten if you had asked fifty people? Did some answers appear in every list? How many were mentioned only once?

"What should Bible teachers know?" There are so many valid answers to this question. Ask it in any crowd of Christians, and you can always count on two answers. "They should know Christ," some will say; and others, "They should know the Bible." Certainly, we can agree on both of those. But I've heard a host of other answers—Christian ethics, church history, systematic theology, missions, church polity, biblical archaeology, educational psychology, human development, principles of counseling, instructional theory, and several others. And not one of these is irrelevant to the work of the Bible teacher. You could also contend that Bible teachers ought to know something about public speaking and discussion group techniques, and that they ought to be in touch with such resources as Christian art, music drama, and literary classics. And shouldn't they have a knowledge of Bible study tools, such as atlases, concordances, theological wordbooks, Bible dictionaries and encyclopedias, and center-column references? The list could go on and on. Where do you draw the line?

While acknowledging that all of these suggestions are valid, and some quite essential, I have tried to reduce the material in this chapter to manageable proportions by focusing on three areas of knowledge—biblical knowledge, knowledge of learners, and knowledge of teaching principles. In other words, the teacher needs to be knowledgeable about the "what," "who," and "how" of teaching.

The second difficulty to which I referred earlier has to do with one potential reaction to the appeals for knowledge contained in this chapter. Occasionally, when I discuss this subject with groups of teachers, someone will say, "If a teacher has to know all of that, I'm going to quit teaching, because I'm not qualified." It's a natural reaction, of course; but it comes from a misunderstanding of my intention. Please view the suggestions in this chapter as a guide for further development, not as a measuring stick for determining who is qualified and who is not. Some of the finest Bible teachers I have ever known had little understanding of teaching principles and, in some respects, were even naive about the Bible. What they lacked in these areas of knowledge, however, they made up for by their dynamic personal faith. It would have been silly to suggest that they were unqualified to serve as Bible teachers. But, on the other hand, their effectiveness could have been greatly enlarged through continued growth in knowledge in these areas.

The Teacher's Biblical Knowledge

Some observers feel that Bible knowledge is sadly lacking even in our churches today. Some Christians hunger to know more about the Bible, and they constantly feed their souls on the Scriptures. But, regrettably, they are few in number. There are literally hundreds of men and women in the church who could not name four Gospels, or four Old Testament prophets, or locate the books of Habakkuk or Philemon if their lives depended on it. And they would be totally confused if asked to locate the Ten Commandments, or the Beatitudes, or Paul's great chapter on love. Unfortunately,

I have seen even Sunday School teachers who could not site a single passage of Scripture having to do with the nature of God or the doctrine of the Holy Spirit.

Whatever else might be said on the subject, let it be said simply, but forcefully, Christian teachers must know the Bible. There is no substitute for biblical knowledge, and there is no excuse for the lack of it. Not every teacher can be vivacious, persuasive, physically attractive, intellectually gifted, or verbally fluent. But every teacher can have biblical knowledge. Not every teacher can be a highly trained Bible scholar, but every teacher can know more about the Bible tomorrow than he or she knew today.

If teachers themselves are casual about the message which they are commissioned to teach, how great will be the scriptural darkness. "Can the blind lead the blind? shall they not both fall into the ditch?" (Luke 6:39). But, so long as there are faithful men and women who love the Bible enough to study it diligently and teach it correctly, there is some hope that we will see a renewal of biblical knowledge in our time.

Rightly handling the word of truth. "Study to show thyself approved unto God, a workman that needeth not to be ashamed, rightly dividing the word of truth" (2 Tim. 2:15). This word of encouragement to the young pastor Timothy ought to be every Bible teacher's motto. The Revised Standard Version translates it: "Do your best to present yourself to God as one approved, a workman who has no need to be ashamed, rightly handling the word of truth." The message is clear. It is not enough for us to handle the word of truth; we are under divine obligation to handle it rightly. We are not to be content to offer just any plausible interpretation of Scriptures; we are to do our best to find the correct interpretation.

Dr. A. T. Robertson, who once taught New Testament

at The Southern Baptist Theological Seminary, Louisville, Kentucky, is reported to have quipped on one occasion: "One certain proof of the Bible's inspiration is that it has withstood more than 3,000 years of preaching." The humor in that statement comes from the fact that there is so much truth in it. Over the centuries the message of the Bible has been twisted, distorted, perverted, misunderstood, watered down, beefed up, and modified in a thousand ways. How else do you explain the fact that Adolf Hitler, one of the most demonic personalities of modern times, and Nikita Kruschev, a professed atheist, could both quote the Bible when it suited their purposes? How else is it possible for racial segregationists and staunch integrationists to find support for their divergent views in the same Bible?

My son, a paper carrier, was making his monthly collections one day and became entangled in a long conversation with a man who fancied himself to be a great interpreter of the Scripture. What my son heard was forty-five minutes worth of half-truths and distortions. Casting about for biblical excuses to support what he had already made up his mind to believe, the man insisted that Isaiah 28 was all about "speaking in tongues" and "being slain in the Spirit." The passage declares that the Lord will speak to his people "by men of strange lips and with an alien tongue," and it tells of those who will "fall backward, and be broken, and snared, and taken" (vv. 11,13, RSV). This, the man said, was a reference to people who were so overcome by the "infilling of the Spirit" that they fell upon the floor in a state of unconsciousness. How sad, to distort the meaning of Scripture so, when but a simple reading of this chapter reveals that the prophet is dealing with the problem of corrupt, drunken priests. They fall down because they are so sodden with wine.

The tragedy of this story is that this man was a Sunday School teacher in a large local church. Only heaven knows how many perversions of truth he has peddled to unsuspecting children over the years. The problem was not so much that he wasn't sincere. Misguided sincerity can be much more dangerous than passive indifference. His problem is that he wasn't diligent enough, or honest enough, to interpret the Word of truth accurately.

There are a great many people who erroneously believe that the Bible is, somehow, just too mysterious to be interpreted with any degree of certainty. So they gullibly accept the notion that "anybody's guess is as good as the next person's," when it comes to deciphering the meaning of Scripture. (You know, "everyone to his own belief.") That attitude sounds democratic, but it isn't in touch with the realities of Bible interpretation. The Bible's message was, and is, divinely inspired; it is an intelligible message meant to be understood and acted upon. And its meaning is available to those who are willing to study it faithfully. Undeniably, there are passages which are difficult to understand, where the test is uncertain and the language puzzling. But these are the exception, not the rule. The Bible teacher should approach the Scriptures confident in the belief that God intends for his Word to be understood.

The historical approach to Bible interpretation. The surest way to interpret a Bible passage accurately is to anchor it in the historical situation that produced it. The biblical message extends to all generations; but it was originated in a particular place and at a particular time. Before the message was written, it was experienced in the arena of human affairs.

The Word of the Lord came to Moses out of a burning bush near Mount Horeb in a living experience. Moses saw with his eyes and heard with his ears; perhaps even feeling the heat of the fire on his face. What he heard had to do with a real event on the stage of history. "I have seen the affliction of my people who are in Egypt," said the Lord (Ex. 3:7, RSV). Apart from that historical setting, neither the message nor the response of Moses makes any sense. Only later was that revelation turned into the written revelation which you have in your Bible.

The Word of the Lord came to Hosea in the midst of an agonizing personal crisis. His wife had violated their relationship, engaging in flagrant acts of adultery, and finally deserting him. As Hosea sat amidst the ruins of his family life, in pain and despair, the Word of the Lord came to him. The message in effect was, "As Gomer has forsaken you, Hosea, so has Israel forsaken the living God." Precisely because he had experienced the pain of rejected love in his own life, Hosea understood the agony in the heart of God. The experienced Word became the spoken Word, as this prophet preached to his generation; then, much later, it became a written word.

The Word of the Lord came to first-century disciples in the person of Jesus of Nazareth. They walked with him along the dusty roads of Galilee, shared meals with him in the fields and in the houses of friends, and listened to his teachings. Later, they translated their experience with the Incarnate Word into the written Word which we read in the pages of the New Testament. The opening words of 1 John summarize it beautifully: "That which was from the beginning, which we have heard, which we have seen with our eyes, which we have looked upon and touched with our hands, concerning the word of life . . . that which we have seen and heard we proclaim also to you" (1 John 1:1,3, RSV).

Biblical revelation is inspired of God and rooted in history. To ignore the first fact is to deny the essential character of the Scriptures as the channel of God's self-disclosure to his people. To ignore the second fact is to let the meaning of Scripture become subservient to shallow speculation.

There are three basic steps in a historical approach to Bible interpretation. First, you seek to determine what the writer meant to say to his original hearers in the light of their own historical situation. Second, you identify truths which are not bound to that particular historical setting; principles which have universal significance. Third, you answer the question, "What do these truths mean in my situation?"

Let's take a simple example. Turn to Philemon in your New Testament. Read this short epistle. It shouldn't take more than five minutes. Most interpreters agree that Paul wrote this letter in behalf of a slave, Onesimus, who had run away from his owner, Philemon. Onesimus apparently had been converted and had stayed for a while with Paul. But now the apostle was sending this Christian slave back to his master, also a Christian, with this letter in hand. This is a brief summary of the historical situation.

Divorced from its historical setting, this letter says little more than, "Be nice to my friend when he comes to see you." But, placed in its historical context, this letter takes on dramatic ethical significance. For, when we take these circumstances into account, we realize that Paul is risking the very life of Onesimus by sending him back to his master, wagering everything on his belief that Philemon will respond with Christian love and forgiveness, not with anger and vengeance. What if he has guessed wrong? What if Philemon feels compelled to make an example of Onesimus, so as to discourage other escape attempts? The punishment of runaway slaves could be brutal.

But let's remember the second basic step in interpretation.

Can we learn from this epistle only that Christian masters
ought to be kind to runaway slaves; or is there a truth here
that leaps the bounds of its first-century setting? There is
such a message here, similar to that profound statement
in Galatians: "There is neither Jew nor Greek, there is neither bond or free, there is neither male nor female; for ye
are all one in Christ Jesus" (Gal. 3:28, RSV). Whatever else
the relationship between Christians, the dominant relationship is their mutual status as brothers and sisters in Christ.
And the guiding principle in this relationship is love.

Now, how do you take the third step in interpretation?
How do we apply this message to our own historical circum-
stance? Are there any slaveowners in your Bible class? Probably not. But perhaps there are fathers and mothers whose
teenagers have rebelled against parental authority, or man-
agers whose job it is to supervise employees, or school teachers who must deal with recalcitrant students. How would
it affect their relationships if they were to take seriously
the truths implied in Paul's letter to Philemon?

It is true that some Scriptures seem clear enough quite
apart from their immediate historical context. The Golden
Rule, in Matthew 7:12, is one example. However, some passages which seem understandable at first glance take on even
greater meaning when their historical background is understood. The parable of the good Samaritan (Luke 10:29-37)
seems clear enough, even to the casual reader. But you can't
grasp its full meaning without taking into account the deep-
seated animosities between Samaritans and Jews in Jesus'
day.

Look at the woods, then the trees. One of the surest ways
to miss the meaning of a passage of Scripture is to ignore
the nature of the book in which it is found. When was it
written? By whom? To whom? For what purpose? What

kind of literature does it contain? What was going on in the world when it was written? What seems to be the main doctrinal themes? Answers to questions like these will greatly clarify the meanings of specific passages.

The book of Revelation provides a good example of this principle. Revelation was written by a Christian named John who was exiled on the island of Patmos toward the end of first century A.D., and it was almost certainly written either during a time when Romans were persecuting Christians or a time when such a persecution seemed imminent. Most significantly, it was written in the form of apocalyptic literature, which is full of strange symbolism. In apocalyptic, numbers often take on symbolic meaning. For example, the number seven typically stands for "completeness." This is an important key to understanding the frequent repetition of this number—seven churches, seven spirits, seven seals, seven trumpets, seven visions, seven angels, seven bowls, and so on—in the book of Revelation. It is very doubtful that anyone will get very far in his understanding of Revelation without having such background knowledge.

But where does one find such information? There are two or three possible sources. Any good Bible commentary has an introductory section which provides information about the book of the Bible which it is interpreting. One-volume commentaries have an introductory article for each Bible book. Bible encyclopedias and dictionaries also contain such information. Some of these are multivolume reference sets, and some are complete in one volume. The larger sets usually have the greatest amount of information, of course. A few reference Bibles contain short introductions to the books of the Bible.

Armed with information about the historical background of a biblical book, we are in a much better position to interpret specific passages. Suppose one is studying Hosea, for instance, and comes across the several references to "Baal" and "the Baals." Baal worship was very much a part of Hosea's historical situation; and it is impossible to understand his prophetic utterances without some knowledge of Baal worship. Only if one knows that Baal was a fertility god, and was supposed to have the power to bring abundant harvests, can he appreciate the biting irony of Hosea 2:8, "And she did not know that it was I (the true God of Israel) who gave her the grain, the wine, and the oil, and who lavished upon her silver and gold which they used for Baal" (RSV).

This general knowledge of the books of the Bible provides indispensable background information. But, of course, we will need additional data to interpret specific passages. In Revelation 13, we find a bizarre description of a beast which has come out of the sea; and in chapter 17 there is another reference to this same beast. In a commentary, we find the suggestion that this "sea beast" is a symbol of the Roman Empire; and the writer of the commentary gives several plausible reasons for this interpretation. Much of the Roman Empire's political, military, and economic power came to her by way of the sea. But even more to the point is John's identification of the beast's seven heads as "seven hills on which the woman is seated" (17:9). The commentator quite logically interprets this to mean the city of Rome on its legendary seven hills.

Let's look at one other illustration related to the interpretation of Revelation. In connection with his explanation of the letter to Laodicea in Revelation 3:14-22, a commentator provides some interesting historical data. First, Laodicea was noted for her great wealth. Second, Laodicea had a medical school which was widely noted for its famous eye medication.

Third, the city was the center of a thriving garment industry. Against this background, it's easy to see that the taunting statement in 3:17, "you are . . . poor, blind, and naked," is laden with biting sarcasm.

Bible commentaries are the best sources of such information. They come in many varieties. Some are quite large and expensive; some are small and modestly priced, especially those which come in paperbound editions. Some come in multivolume sets; others are single-volume commentaries on single books of the Bible. And there are one-volume commentaries covering all the books of the Bible. Some commentaries are scholarly, quite academic in their approach; others were written for a more popular readership. (You will find specific suggestions on the selection of commentaries and other resources for your own use in the Appendix.)

Using the Bible to interpret the Bible. We are not dependent upon external resources alone when we study the Bible. The Bible often interprets itself. And, fortunately, we have some useful tools to help us dig out this information.

One such tool is the center-column reference found in many editions of the Bible. It consists of a number of Scripture references in a vertical column running down the center of each page. (The references are usually in very fine print.) Some Bibles have similar columns of references printed on the outside edges of the pages; these are called "marginal references," and they serve the same purpose as center-column references.

These references lead you to other Bible passages which help to clarify what is said in the text. I was reading the second chapter of Hebrews the other day and came across the words, "For if the message declared by angels was valid . . ." (v. 2). I stopped and pondered. "Declared by angels? What message was that?" Then I looked at the center-col-

umn reference. It referred to two Scriptures, Acts 7:53 and
Galatians 3:19. Both of these verses say that the law of Moses
was given through angels. The "message declared by angels"
is clearly a reference to the Old Testament law.

On another occasion I was reading the creation account
in Genesis 1 and noticed, at verse 9, a reference to Psalm
104:6-9. Turning to that reference, I discovered that Psalm
104 is really a "creation psalm," amazingly parallel to the
creation narrative in Genesis. Such is the value of a center-
column reference.

The following teaching lab activity will help you to see
how center-column and marginal references work. You will
need a Bible, but it need not contain reference columns.

TEACHING LAB ACTIVITY NO. 10

Turn to the Gospel of John and read 1:1-3. Then
look up each reference in the column below. These
references are arranged exactly as they might appear
in a center-column reference. (Note that *1.1* and *1.3*
are italicized. These refer to verses 1 and 3 of John
1. The Scriptures following each are related to that
verse.) As you look up each reference, jot down a brief
note on its content.

1.1: Gen 1.1:
Col 1.17: 1 Jn
1.1-2: Jn 1.14:
Rev. 19.13:
Jn 17.5;20.28:
1.3 Ps 33.6:
Jn 1.10: 1 Cor
8.6: Col 1.16:
Heb 1.2.

Did you have any trouble locating the reference which is not preceded by the name of a book, 20:28? Or did you guess that this belongs with the preceding reference and, thus, refers to John 20:28?

Running down parallel references like this takes a little time, but the diligent Bible student will be rewarded with some intriguing insights. Isn't it striking that a New Testament Gospel writer takes us back to the scene with which the Bible opened, "In the beginning . . ."? And did you notice that the psalmist (Ps. 33:6) specifically refers to the "word" of the Lord as the agent of creation? How significant that John associates Jesus Christ with this powerful Word through whom the world was brought into being (John 1:1-3,14). And, of course, Colossians 1:16-17 is an explicit statement of this same doctrine.

Now let's take a different example, one in which a passage of Scripture refers to an event in the history of Israel. The Scripture is Hosea 1:4. The center-column reference tells you where to find the historical account to which this verse refers:

1.4: 2 Kings 10.1-14

The passage in 2 Kings certainly helps us to understand the phrase, "blood of Jezreel," doesn't it?

The most useful Bible study tool you can have, in my opinion, is a complete concordance. Many editions of the Bible have small concordances in the back. And these are useful to a limited degree. But here I am thinking about much larger concordances, such as *Cruden's Complete Con-*

cordance to the Bible or *Young's Analytical Concordance*. These contain complete listings of all references in which all the key words of the Bible appear. If Bible teachers could afford to own only one Bible study resource, in addition to the Bible itself, I would advise them to acquire a complete concordance.

A concordance has three main uses. First, when you want to know whether or not a quotation comes from the Bible, you can check this out with the aid of a concordance. Now, let's say that you are trying to find the source of the familiar saying, "A soft answer turneth away wrath." Did it come from the Bible, or was it one of Benjamin's proverbs? Turn in your concordance to the key word "soft," and there it is. Can you spot it in the following list of references from a concordance?

SOFT

> speak *s.* words unto thee?   Job 41:3
> makest it *s.* with showers.   Ps. 65:10
> a *s.* answer turneth away   Prov. 15:1
> *s.* raiment; they that wear *s.* clothing
> Matt. 11:8; Luke 7:25

(Notice that the key word is always abbreviated so as not to waste space by repeating it in full each time.)

Second, a concordance can be useful when you know only part of a biblical quotation, and you want to know how the whole quotation goes. Let's say, for instance, that you are preparing a devotional for a campfire service, and the words, "The heavens declare the glory of God," keep coming to mind. What an appropriate Scripture to use out there under the stars. But what is the rest of that quotation, and where is it found in the Bible? A quick look in your concordance,

under one of the key words "heavens," "declare," "firma-
ment," or "glory" will lead you to the source of the quotation,
Psalm 19:1.

Third, even more importantly, a concordance can be used
as a guide to the study of biblical themes, such as "love,"
"righteousness," "forgiveness," "law," "salvation," or "judgment."

I once was preparing to lead a study of 1 Corinthians
13, Paul's great chapter on Christian love. *What a demanding thing it is to practice such love,* I thought, *where does
one find the ability to live this kind of life?* Thinking that
the Bible itself might hold some answers to this question,
I used a concordance to locate a number of Scriptures on
the subject of love. One of these was Romans 5:5, which
provided a clear answer to the question. "God's love has
been poured into our hearts through the Holy Spirit which
has been given to us" (RSV). And I also found a less direct
but meaningful clue in Luke 7:47, where Jesus indicates
that a great sense of forgiveness produces great love in one's
heart, and that "he who is forgiven little, loves little." What
a great insight that one's desire to live a life of Christian
love is directly proportionate to one's sense of forgiveness
in Christ!

You probably have noticed my references to commentaries, Bible dictionaries, concordances, and center-column
references as "Bible study tools." And that's exactly what
they are. You don't study them. You work with them as
you study the Bible. They are means to an end, not ends
within themselves. And I would include church lesson materials and teacher's commentaries in this same category. I
want to make a point of this, because I fear that some people
tend to make a fetish of certain Bible study tools. There
are teachers, for instance, who latch onto a favorite Sunday

School lesson commentary, buy a new edition of that same commentary each year, and study nothing else. And there are some who hold their reference Bibles in such awe that they tend to forget that the comments and notes in them are not part of the inspired text. The teacher's goal ought to be to gain a greater knowledge of the Bible itself, using with gratitude all the study tools available.

Developing a reservoir of Bible knowledge. This will sound silly, but can you imagine going to a doctor who, having no general knowledge of medicine, has to "bone up" on each ailment brought into his office? Picture yourself sitting on an examining table and hearing the doctor say, "That looks like a plantar wart on your heel; I'll try to remove it just as soon as I read up on how to do it." Worse still, imagine yourself lying on an operating table looking up at a surgeon who is engrossed in a book, *How to Perform an Appendectomy in Five Easy Steps.*

Farfetched? Well, yes. But no more so than the notion that a Bible teacher can do his job that way, boning up on the Bible passage for each specific lesson without giving much attention to more fundamental Bible study. Some may get by that way for a while, but their teaching will soon wear thin. Good Bible teachers teach "out of the overflow" of their biblical knowledge. That expression is old and hackneyed, I know. But it aptly describes what I am talking about. A Bible teacher needs to have a reservoir of general Bible knowledge, not just a little canteen full for each session.

At this point, I can hear some reader saying, "I'm reading this book because I'm strictly new at this job. I hardly know what to teach or how to teach it; and, now, this guy wants me to be an encyclopedia of Bible knowledge." Believe me, I am sympathetic with the person who has never had much opportunity to study the Bible in depth but, in spite of that, is trying to work at a full-time vocation, run a household, and do a respectable job as a Bible teacher.

OK. So maybe you're not a walking library of biblical knowledge just now. And you're not going to become one overnight. But you can make a beginning. Don't worry about what you don't know. Just think about what you can learn today, and tomorrow, and the next day, with consistent effort. And that word, *consistent*, is the big one. There's a fellow in Kentucky who taught himself French in the thirty minutes a day he spent walking to and from work. It took him four years; but he learned French.

The important thing is to have a plan, a program of personal Bible study. I wouldn't begin to suggest that there is a single plan that will suit everybody's needs. But I can give you an example. Several years ago, in a seminary classroom, I heard a professor say that he tried to do a depth study of one book of the Bible at a time, averaging about two books every year. And that's the plan I have tried to follow in my own personal Bible study. This sometimes fits in nicely with a three- or six-month study of a book in my own Bible class; sometimes I develop an interest in a particular book for other reasons. One advantage of this plan is that it gives me an excuse to pick up a good commentary or two as I concentrate on each book. I don't try to hold to a rigid schedule; I simply stay with a book for as long as it takes to get a reasonably good grasp of it.

If you use a plan like this, don't feel compelled to move through the Bible from beginning to end, starting with Genesis and going through Revelation. Alternate studies in the Old Testament with studies in the New testament. For example, Genesis, the Gospel of John, Exodus, and Acts would be a good sequence to begin with.

Unless you are already fairly knowledgeable about the

Bible, you probably would profit from reading some general background information on the nature of the Bible, principles of Bible interpretation, and various kinds of Bible study helps. One source of such information is a sixty-four-page booklet which I prepared a few years ago entitled *Developing Skills for Bible Interpretation.* This booklet, written in a self-study format, is available from the Sunday School Board of the Southern Baptist Convention, 127 Ninth Avenue, North, Nashville, Tennessee 37234. The cost is very modest. (Other resources of this kind are listed in the Appendix.)

You might be lucky enough to live in an area where group Bible study opportunities are available through church-related college or seminary extension courses. My own denomination (Southern Baptist) maintains a Seminary Extension Department (460 James Robertson Parkway, Nashville, Tennessee 37219) which offers classes at centers throughout the United States. And, for those who do not live near these centers, this department offers an extensive correspondence study curriculum.

Whatever approach you choose, promise yourself that Bible study will be a priority item in your life. Not only will it be personally rewarding; it will also enable you to teach the Scriptures with confidence, freedom, and enthusiasm, "rightly dividing the word of truth."

The Teacher's Knowledge of Learners

Back in the early 1960's I was a doctoral student in the field of religious education; so, naturally, I spoke very authoritatively whenever I appeared before a group of church teachers. One summer evening I was making my standard speech about "Knowing the Learner," assuring my audience, with great conviction, that they were destined to be miserable failures if they did not take pains to know something about the people who sat under their teaching week by week. "Why?" asked a voice from the back row. "Why is it so necessary for me to know my class members?" The question came from a young man who, being a college English teacher, was inclined to be irreverent toward doctoral students in religious education. He went on to insist that he always did a quite respectable job of preparing and presenting his Bible lessons, and that being better acquainted with his class members wouldn't change the way he did it.

His question took me by surprise, since "understanding the learner" was a sacred principle which I thought everyone took for granted. But I have been grateful ever since that he dared to challenge that assumption, because it made me give a lot more attention to the matter. And, today, what was then an unexamined assumption has become an unshakable conviction. You can "present lessons," but you can't teach people very effectively unless you know something about them. There are three reasons for this conviction. First, teaching and learning is a transaction, like selling and buying. (You can be very sure that a good salesman isn't going to be indifferent to the thoughts, attitudes, and needs of his customer.) Second, you must meet learners where they are, not where you wish them to be. Third, the biblical message becomes living truth for the learner where it touches his or her personal experience; therefore, it is important for the teacher to be aware of the personal experience of the learner as well as to have knowledge of the biblical message.

The teaching-learning transaction. Some religious educators are fond of saying, "You don't teach the Bible; you teach persons." It's a neat little cliché; but it's only a half-truth.

The truth is, you teach both the Bible and persons. You must keep both of these elements in the teaching-learning transaction in proper tension.

We use the term "transaction" to indicate an exchange involving two persons. If a saleslady comes to your door and shows some products, you wouldn't call that a transaction. But if you give her money in exchange for the products, that would be a transaction. Even the giving and receiving of a gift is a transaction. It involves two persons; a giver and a receiver. I can't give you anything unless you are willing to receive it. Teaching and learning are two sides of the same transaction. It takes two persons to complete it.

Let's carry the analogy between selling-and-buying and teaching-and-learning a bit further. A good insurance salesman must be thoroughly acquainted with what he is selling; but he must also know as much as possible about his customer. He must take into account his customer's family, occupation, income, financial assets, age, health, and the current status of his insurance program. If he is experienced and really knows his business, he doesn't just deliver a stereotyped sales pitch. He tailors his presentation to his customer's needs and interests. And the Bible teacher must function in much the same way.

The message obviously must take into account the age of the learner. "Honor thy father and thy mother" has quite different meanings to the seventeen-year-old who feels a strong need to assert her personal independence and the fifty-year-old whose aging father can no longer care for himself. But many other factors—such as occupation, educational background, marital status, and religious experience—have a bearing on the learner's reception of the biblical message.

Consider the meaning of Ephesians 5:22, which says,

"Wives, submit yourselves unto your own husbands, as unto the Lord." Do you think this will be heard in precisely the same manner by the woman who has a beautiful marriage, and the woman whose alcoholic husband spends all his wages at the local tavern and constantly abuses his family?

Ephesians 6:4 is a wonderful admonition for young parents, but what are single adults supposed to make of this? The exhortation of James, "visit the fatherless and widows" (1:27) seems clear enough to those whose family circles are unbroken still; but what about children and youth who have no fathers and women who *are* widows?

"Not forsaking the assembling of ourselves together" (Heb. 10:25) means "don't neglect church attendance" to most people; but how does the woman who must constantly care for an invalid mother at home respond to this scriptural injunction?

The example of Zaccheus—"Behold, Lord, the half of my goods I give to the poor" (Luke 19:8)—presents a powerful challenge to the class member who has a six-digit annual income; but what does it say to the person who is too disabled to work and is living on welfare checks?

The point of all of this is that the message is shaped not just by the teacher's understanding of it, but also by the learner's hearing of it. And the learner's hearing of it will be influenced by a number of elements in his personality and his everyday experience. So, if the teacher is interested in what the learner is hearing—what he is getting out of the message—he must be in touch with the personal experience of the learner.

Meeting learners where they are. A number of years ago I visited a Sunday School class in a small, struggling church in an inner-city neighborhood. Most of the people were poor, undereducated, and inexperienced in the Christian life. The young woman who was teaching the class explained, half apologetically, "What we do in our class this morning may not resemble Bible study very much. But we're making some progress. Two months ago our members couldn't even talk with one another. Everyone just came and sat without saying a word." She started the class by asking, "Well, how did your week go? Did anyone have any interesting experiences?" One by one, the class members shared experiences with one another, most of them mundane and run-of-the-mill. But they responded to one another, and everyone seemed to enjoy it. And, sure enough, little more than fifteen minutes were spent on the Bible lesson itself.

This young woman was very wise. It would have been a waste of time to have launched into a lecture on the divided kingdom of Israel or the doctrine of the Logos in the prologue to the Fourth Gospel. Her class members were not ready for that. Their situation was not unlike that on a foreign mission field. Without much background in Bible study, they could handle only the most rudimentary scriptural teachings. So their teacher met them at their level. The important point is that she was able to do this because she understood her class members. She had visited in their homes; talked with them on the streets; learned something about their values, interests, and workaday experiences.

Admittedly, this is an extreme example. Not every Bible class is so limited in Bible background and social experience. But the need for teachers to be in touch with their class members is just as urgent on the other end of the socioeconomic spectrum. Ernest J. Loessner, who was first my professor and later my colleague, did an intensive study of adult Bible classes during his graduate work at Indiana University. He conducted numerous interviews with teachers and their class members. One woman, well-educated and affluent, the wife of a successful physician, said to him: "Our teacher is one of the sweetest Christians you will find anywhere. But she doesn't really know her class members. She needs to quit thinking of us as angels, and start thinking of us as the devils we really are."

Have you ever noticed how often the Gospels tell us that Jesus knew what was in the thoughts and hearts of the people around him? (Read Matt. 9:4; 12:25; Luke 6:8; 9:47; John 2:25; 6:61; and 16:19. I used a concordance to look these up, by the way.) This was not some kind of magic, not a mind-reading trick. Jesus had a penetrating perception of the thoughts and motives of people because he cared for them deeply and observed them carefully. Others in that crowd at Jericho (Luke 19:1-3) could have seen the loneliness and alienation of a man like Zacchaeus, but they ignored him. Jesus saw because he cared. He stopped in the middle of that throng and focused his attention fully on Zacchaeus. When a sinful woman washed and anointed the feet of Jesus in the house of Simon the Pharisee, Simon *said to himself,* "If this man were a prophet, he would have known who and what sort of a woman this is who is touching him, for she is a sinner" (Luke 7:39, RSV). And Jesus responded to Simon's private thoughts, teaching him a great lesson in the relationship between forgiveness and love (Luke 7:40-47). Was Jesus a mind reader? Or was it that he was so sensitive to the thought patterns and motives of this Pharisee that he could quickly perceive what his reaction would be to a situation like this? He knew where Simon's thoughts were, and he engaged him at that point.

The Bible teacher will often be called upon to do just that; to meet individuals where they are in their thinking, their attitudes, their perceptions of things. A teacher of women can't lead a study of Matthew 5:27-32, surely, without being sensitive to the fact that there are four divorcees sitting in the class. A teacher cannot ignore the relevance of Ephesians 2:13-22 to pronounced racist attitudes held by some class members. Following the example of the Master Teacher, today's Bible study leader must "perceive the thoughts of their hearts."

Where the Bible touches life. Some schools today offer courses in what they call the "objective study of the Bible," which means that the Bible is treated as great literature or as a reference book for the study of religions. And this is all right, I suppose; but I've never gotten very excited about its potential. For the Bible wasn't written to be studied objectively. It was written to inspire, to convict, to call the unredeemed to repentance. It's message is intended to penetrate to the very core of the reader's being. "For the word of God is quick, and powerful, and sharper than any two-edged sword, piercing even to the dividing asunder of soul and spirit, and of the joints and marrow, and is a discerner of the thoughts and intents of the heart" (Heb. 4:12).

The written word becomes a living word for the learner when it mingles with the raw materials of his daily existence; his likes and dislikes, his work and leisuretime activities, his affectionate relationships. To teach without firsthand knowledge of the lives of learners is to fire scatter-loads of biblical truth, hoping that they will find a mark somewhere. To know the learner is to have the ability to pinpoint those places where revealed truth intersects with personal experience.

One of the most effective Bible teachers I know makes it a point to be acquainted with the men in his class. One day he was leading the class, a group of professionals and businessmen, in a study of Matthew 26:30-46, the story of Jesus in Gethsemane. Commenting on verse 40, where Jesus exclaims, "What! Could you not watch with me one hour?" the teacher made a practical application. "What was happening here?" he asked. "We might say that Jesus was losing his personal support system, just when he needed to be able to count on it. Whether we realize it or not, each of us needs a personal support system—a group of people who really care for us—especially when we go through bad times." Then, he turned to a man in the class, an executive who had lost his job in a corporate merger, and asked: "Jim, did you have a personal support system to fall back on when you were suddenly hit by a career crisis a few weeks ago?" This opened the door to an intensely personal and deeply meaningful discussion among the men in this fellowship of learning.

A teacher who doesn't know anything about his class members would never ask a question like that, for two reasons. In the first place, he wouldn't be that much in touch with what was going on in the lives of members. But, more importantly, he would not have the kind of personal relationship that gives one a right to ask such questions.

Adding a personal dimension to your teaching will greatly enlarge your personal ministry to class members and, at the same time, deepen their understanding of the Bible's message. Jan helped me to understand this that day in the hospital, when her baby was so sick. I still remember that isolation sign on the door of the room. It told me to expect the worst. I knocked softly and Jan came to the door, stepping out into the hall. The baby had meningitis. The diagnosis was positive. But the doctors were hoping against hope that the lab report would give them some cause for optimism. I went away with a heavy heart. But how things had changed by the next day! Jan was beaming when she met me at the door this time. The meningitis had turned out to be a fairly mild, noncontagious form of the disease, and the baby had already begun to respond to the antibiotics the doctors had prescribed for her.

"Can you stay for a few minutes?" Jan asked. "I want to talk with you about something." I went in and sat on a stool near the chair Jan had slept in all night. "Do you remember that lesson," she asked, "the one about the nature of God, just a few weeks ago?" I nodded. "I didn't say much that day," she went on, "but I wanted so much to tell you that I didn't agree with what you were saying." I was filled with curiosity.

Then Jan told me that she had never been able to think of God as a loving, tender Father. "All my life I've thought of him as sort of an angry God," she said, "one who was ready to punish you if you stepped out of line." She paused momentarily. "But now I know differently," she said softly. "Because as I've sat here in this dark room the last two nights, God has been close to me and comforted me. And I know that he loves me." For several minutes more we sat talking about her experience with God. And I shared with her some of my experiences, and some of my beliefs. When I finally got up to leave, we both knew that God had revealed himself more clearly to both of us. In experiences like that, Bible study takes on its deepest meaning.

How to study learners. Let's assume, for the moment, that my appeal for knowledge of the learner has taken root. How does a teacher acquire such knowledge? I suggest a two-level approach, the first general and the second more particular. On the general level, teachers ought to know something about the age group which they teach. On the particular level, teachers should make it a point to know the individuals in their classes.

If you are teaching senior adults, for instance, there are

books on older adulthood which would be well worth the reading. The same is true for middle-aged adults, young marrieds, single adults, or youth. Materials of this kind are usually called "developmental studies," simply because they grow out of research on human development in different age categories.

(You will find a list of such books included in the Appendix.)

Developmental studies will help you to become more alert to experiences which are common to people at various stages of life. Sometimes these will bring into sharper focus what you have already learned through experience; and sometimes they will provide valuable new information. For example, you might have already learned through experience how much time and energy (and money?) must be invested in courtship and early engagement; something which all teachers of single adults ought to keep in mind. But perhaps you have not been aware of the increasing number of studies which are radically altering our previous perceptions of middle adulthood. At one time it was thought that middle age was normally one of the most stable, harmonious periods of adulthood, a stage in which most persons managed to "put it all together." But more recent research indicates that this may well be one of the most difficult, crisis-ridden periods of life.

What has this to do with Bible teaching? It's a fair question. Let's answer it with some examples.

One Wednesday evening at church, the teacher of an older men's Bible class was ranting about an upcoming lesson in the Bible study curriculum. The lesson was on the Commandment, "Thou shalt not commit adultery," and it included some of the teachings of Jesus on the subject ("every one who looks at a woman lustfully has already committed adultery with her in his heart"). "I don't know what this has to do with my class," this teacher complained, "Every man in it has reached retirement age!" I don't know who he was trying to kid; but even if he really was this uninformed, any respectable developmental study of older adulthood could have told him that human beings don't retire their sexuality at sixty-five.

When leading a study of Paul's stirring words in Philippians 3:14, "I press toward the mark for the prize of the high calling of God in Christ Jesus," a teacher of young adults needs to be reminded of all the other marks toward which they are pressing (economic security, educational degrees, career goals, for example).

The story of Abram's call ("Go from your country and your kindred and your father's house to the land that I will show you" v. 1, RSV) in Genesis 12 has a great deal of relevance to the vocational crisis which hits some men and women in their late thirties and their forties. It is not uncommon. You wake up one morning to the shocking realization that more than half your life is gone. The years before you are fewer than the years behind you. And you think, "If I am going to accomplish anything in this life, other than what I am already accomplishing, I'd better get at it." Recent developmental studies of adulthood have shown that it is not at all unusual for men and women to start new careers and make other radical changes at this stage of life. And that, essentially, was what Abram did when he left the security of Haran.

We know some of these things from personal experience, of course. Most of us have observed already that the birth of the first child in a young family calls for a reordering of relationships, that retirement can deal a blow to one's self-esteem and sense of usefulness, and that one of the painful experiences of the aging is the loss of companions and friends. But reading books on human development helps us to think systematically about the life experiences of those who participate in our Bible study groups. And there's an added bonus; lesson illustrations abound in developmental literature, the kinds of illustrations which add personal meaning to Bible study.

But let's think for a while about that other approach to gaining a knowledge of learners, on a more specific level. An automobile owner's manual will fill you in on the standard characteristics of a particular model. But drive a car for two or three years and it will develop characteristics of its own which are definitely not standard. For instance, the manual might caution not to pump the accelerator when you start your car; but you do it anyway because you've discovered through long experience that it's the *only* way to start *your* particular car. Then there's that annoying rattle in the radio speaker which can be cured only by a sharp rap on the dash, and the slight sag in the left rear door which requires you to lift up a bit when you close it. You know how it goes. All cars share general characteristics, but each car has its individual traits. Learners are that way. You can learn a great deal about them by reading books; but you can know an individual only by reading him.

I sometimes ask teachers to participate in an interesting experiment. (I am indebted to Dr. Paul Torrance, well known for his work in creative teaching for the idea.) I'll give each teacher a rock, or stick, or peanut, and ask him or her to study it very carefully. If we are in a conference which lasts several days, I'll ask the teachers to keep these objects during the whole time, continuing to study them as much as possible. Then, later, I'll collect all of them, spread them out on a table, and ask each person to pick out his own rock, stick, or peanut. I have never yet seen a teacher fail to identify an object which she has studied carefully over a period of time.

There is a profound lesson in this for teachers. The first time you go into a classroom, especially if several people are present, you tend to see them as a group rather than as individuals. Just so may faces. But, as you come to know them better as individuals—their attitudes, mannerisms, physical traits, interests, talents, speech patterns, and the like—they take on quite distinctive identities.

We usually carry the experiment one step further. As the teachers study the objects which have been given to them, I ask them to list all the ways in which they could find out more about it. At first, responses are slow. But, as the teachers apply themselves to the task, ideas begin to flow more freely, and they will make suggestions like these:

- Look at it against different backgrounds.
- Look at it under different lighting conditions.
- Compare it to other rocks.
- Weigh it.
- Put it in water.
- Measure it.
- Touch it.
- Smell it.
- Use a hammer and chisel on it.

It is not uncommon for a group of twenty to come up with a hundred or more of these suggestions. Then we discuss this question: "Do these ideas suggest ways in which we might get to know our class members better?" This usually produces a conversation like this:

"We need to look at class members against different backgrounds. We ought to see them in places other than the classroom. Their homes, for instance.

"Yes, and have you noticed what different impressions

of a person you get when she is wearing different kinds of clothes? When you see people dressed in their Sunday best all the time, then see them in old work clothes, it can change your whole attitude toward them."

"Sure. And don't forget that people look different under different lighting conditions, just as rocks do. Any photographer can tell you that."

"I think we are always comparing people to others, don't you? When we say things like, 'Mary is the best Bible student in my class,' we're speaking in comparative terms."

"That suggests another idea to me. We need to put people together, not just to compare them, but to see how they behave in groups. A person who behaves one way in class— let's say he's very quiet, for instance—might be completely different when you get him off to himself."

"I don't think we'll get away with weighing class members, but I do think we get to know something about people when we touch them. You know, even when you shake hands with them, you get an impression of strength, or softness, or warmth; and this contributes to your overall impression of them."

"Does anyone use a hammer and chisel on your class members?"

"Sometimes I have the urge to."

"I chisel away at their prejudices sometimes. And, come to think of it, that's not a bad way to get to know people better. When they're feeling a bit of pressure."

That's how it goes. Teachers can have a good time comparing ideas like this. But it isn't just frivolous play. Such activities can provide important clues for gaining a better knowledge of class members. If you want to know learners better, have personal contacts with them, visit them in their homes and at work, see them during leisure hours, talk with them in private conversation as well as in group discussion, compare them with other members, see how they react under the pressure of competing ideas. All of these can be taken quite seriously as suggestions for studying the individuals whom you teach.

If you really want to make a serious effort to know your class members, you'll find it important to keep systematic records. I would suggest keeping a notebook with a page or two for each member. The chart in teaching Lab Activity No. 11 provides a sample of the kind of information which you might want to keep in such a notebook. A record of this kind should be kept only for the personal use of the teacher, of course. It should not be shared with others.

TEACHING LAB ACTIVITY NO. 11

Instructions: Select a member of your class to serve as a model for the "MEMBER PROFILE" below. (If you are not presently teaching, select someone in the Bible class which you attend.) Fill in the information by writing phrases, sentences, or brief paragraphs under each heading. The words in parentheses under each heading are intended to suggest information which you might want to include. If your present information is incomplete, don't worry about it. You can add it later.

MEMBER PROFILE

MEMBER'S NAME _____

ADDRESS _____

HOME PHONE _____ BUS. PHONE _____

BIRTH DATE _____ OCCUPATION _____

FAMILY

Marital status:

(Never married? Married? Separated or divorced? How long? Widowed? How long? Previous marriages?)

Children:

(How many? Age and sex of each? Special problems?

Parents:

(Living? Where? Special problems?)

RELIGIOUS EXPERIENCE

Relation to Christ:

(Confessing Christian? When and where baptized? Does faith seem vital?)

Church relationship:

(Church member? Where? Attends services regularly? Serves in leadership roles?)

Devotional life:

(Prays in public? Has daily devotionals? Family devotionals?)

Knowledge of Bible:

(Brings Bible to class? Can locate Scripture references? Prepares lesson? Volunteers information about Bible in class?)

EDUCATION

Schooling:

(Diplomas and degrees? What schools? Major subjects?)

Continuing education:

(Recent or current courses? Training programs? Evening school? Adult education courses?)

VOCATION

Present employment:

(Where? Type of work? Work schedule?)

Occupational skills:

(Special training? Previous work experience? Special skills?)

Attitude toward work:
(Happy or unhappy? Would like change in jobs? Long-range vocational plans?)

HEALTH
General condition:
(Weight? Strength? Energy? Hearing? Sight?)

Special health problems:
(Chronic diseases? Physical handicaps? Hospitalizations?)

RELATIONSHIPS
Friends:
(Many or few friendships? Who are closest friends?)

Affirmations:
(Club memberships? Fraternal organizations? Professional associations? Unions?)

ATTITUDES
Values:
(What things are important to this member? What does he/she especially like or value?)

Negative attitudes:
(Strong dislikes? Negative feelings? Prejudices or biases?)

NEEDS
What are the greatest needs of this member?
(Social? Emotional? Intellectual? Spiritual? Economic? Physical?)

Teachers occasionally raise questions about the kind of written record suggested above. They are reasonable questions, and deserve to be dealt with seriously. So, let me give you the three questions most frequently raised, along with my answers to them:

Question: "Isn't information like this very personal? Won't my class members tell me that these things are none of my business?"

Answer: "Yes. It is very personal. But so is Bible teaching. How can you challenge members to repent of sins, give up prejudices, change their values, serve one another in love, aspire to higher standards, and follow Christ more closely, without getting personal? To rob Bible study of its personal dimension is to make it sterile and insipid. Members won't tell you that these things are none of your business, because you will never ask them these questions directly. The teacher doesn't say, 'By the way, have you any prejudices or needs?'; but, rather, draws conclusions based on observation of what the member says and does. This record is simply a teacher's way of talking with herself about members."

Question: "How can I possibly find time to do all of this record keeping? I barely have enough time to prepare the lesson each week?"

Answer: "This question implies that being knowledgeable about *what* is taught is more important than being knowledgeable about *who* is taught. As you know, I don't share this assumption."

Question: "I have so many class members, I could never complete this information on all of them."

Answer: "This is one of the best arguments I know for having small classes. When the membership of a Bible class grows beyond twenty-five, the teacher tends not to be in touch with learners on a personal basis; interpersonal communication gives way to mass communication."

Before we conclude this discussion on knowing learners,

I want to invite you to try the experiment described earlier; the one done with rocks, sticks, or peanuts. The instructions in the next teaching lab activity will tell you how to proceed.

TEACHING LAB ACTIVITY NO. 12

To kick off this activity, pick up a pebble somewhere, then carry out the following instructions:

1. Examine the pebble as carefully as possible, noting its shape, weight, texture, color, and unique markings. Ask yourself questions, such as: "Where did it come from? How old is it? What is it made of? What is it good for? What is it like?"

2. Carry the pebble with you wherever you go for a whole week. Take it out and examine it whenever you have an opportunity.

3. Sit down with the pebble in front of you and write as many answers as possible to this questions: "How could I find out more about this pebble?" What could you do with it or to it? What instruments could you use on it? Where could you get more information about it? Don't settle for four or five answers; try to list at least twenty.

4. Now look at your list of answers and ask another question: "Do the items on this list suggest ways of knowing my class members better?" Write down any ideas that occur to you.

5. Put your pebble on a table with about two dozen other pebbles and see if you can pick it out from among the others.

(*Note:* You can do this activity alone. But it will be more enjoyable, and probably more instructive, if you can get two or three other persons to participate in it, too.)

The Teacher's Knowledge of Teaching

This chapter began with the question, "What do teachers need to know?" Thus far, we've looked at two areas of knowledge, Bible knowledge (what we teach) and knowledge of learners (who we teach). Now let's turn our attention to principles of teaching (how we teach).

No one can give you a list of instructions labeled "How to Teach in Ten Easy Steps" and expect you to follow them as you would a recipe. Even cooking doesn't work that way. Three cooks can follow the same recipe and turn out three quite different dishes. Every cook has a distinctive style and so has every teacher. But just as there are generally accepted rules for cooking, there are principles which are generally regarded as dependable guidelines for teaching.

Many of these principles could just as well be called "principles of learning," since teaching and learning are so closely intermingled. Suppose, just for the sake of illustration, we could say: "People learn better on Tuesdays." That obviously would be a principle of learning. But, without much modification, we could turn that into a principle of teaching: "For maximum learning, teach people on Tuesdays."

I won't try to present a complete list of teaching principles here, because that's what the next four chapters are about. We've touched on some of them, in fact. But I would like to offer five examples of such principles, to illustrate what "principles of teaching" are like.

A sampler of teaching principles. A discussion of the principles of teaching can produce many differences of opinion. Many questions related to that subject are yet unsettled. But I think it can fairly be said that most educators would agree with the following generalizations:

1. *People will try harder to learn when the learning gives them pleasure, satisfies needs, or promises to be useful.*

Sometimes it isn't very hard to motivate learners. Most teenagers will work hard to learn how to drive a car, for instance. Why? Because they love it. This learning activity is rewarding in itself. And it satisfies important needs. The need to find approval in the eyes of friends. The need to master skills generally associated with adulthood. And, obviously, driving promises to be a useful skill. So, here we have an example of a learning task which involves all three of the motives mentioned above.

But it isn't always that easy. Studying the prophecy of Malachi might not be that exciting. But it doesn't have to be dull either. One way to generate interest is to use a variety of learning methods. Some learners will become engrossed in problem-solving activities in the classroom for the same reason that they will spend an hour or two on a crossword puzzle at home. Storytelling enthralls learners of all ages. Creative activities, role playing, and just old-fashioned group conversation provide a lot of built-in satisfaction for most people.

Remember, too, that people are more likely to throw themselves into learning tasks when they speak to their personal needs. Studies of adult education programs have shown that many enroll because learning groups satisfy social needs—the need to be with other people, to exchange ideas, and to work with others toward common goals. Group discussions and team projects are good methods for processing information; but, more than that, they provide opportunities for fellowship.

And, speaking of the satisfaction of personal needs, we must not forget that many of the members of our Bible classes are there because they find spiritual nurture in the study of Scripture. They are like the psalmist who wrote, "How sweet are thy words to my taste, sweeter than honey to my mouth! Through thy precepts I get understanding" (Ps. 119:103-104, RSV).

People tend to take greater interest in study activities when the result promises to be useful in their daily lives. Have you ever stopped to think about the many members of your own church who never participate in Bible study of any kind? No doubt, there are a number of reasons for this; but one problem is that some folks literally "don't see any use of it." They can't see how Bible study could have any bearing on everyday experience. Maybe this attitude is a sign of spiritual dullness. But, then again, we must consider the fact that the Bible has so often been taught as just a monotonous recital of ancient history, or as a patchwork quilt of morality stories.

Is biblical knowledge not useful in the arena of everyday life? Ask the assembly-line worker in Louisville, who because of his consistent Christian life, spends almost every lunch hour counseling fellow workers who come to him with personal problems. Ask the father whose college-age son wants to know, "Just what's so wrong with homosexuality, anyway?" Or ask the mother whose seventeen-year-old daughter, recovering from an overdose of sleeping pills, looks her in the eye and says, "Give me one good reason why I should want to go on living." The Bible teacher is constantly challenged to find ways to demonstrate the vital relationship of biblical revelation to the issues of everyday life. We don't have to "make the Bible relevant." It is already relevant. Out task is to make this fact clear to learners.

2. *In learning groups, the level of participation is higher when teaching activities are directed to the whole person.*

Some teachers apparently don't think of learners in the classroom as whole persons. They look upon them as ears mounted on legs, because all they do is talk to their ears.

They do not engage their eyes, except incidentally, with a few gestures or facial expressions. They do not engage their minds, for they give them nothing to think about. They do not engage their feelings, for the whole process is virtually devoid of emotion. And they certainly do not call upon their powers of speech, since talk in their classrooms is a one-way street.

This principle means that teaching-learning methods should engage the learner as a complete physical-psychological-spiritual being. For example, in leading a study of Isaiah 6, the teacher will be mindful of the fact that class members need something more than an exposition of a prophet's encounter with the living God; they need to encounter the living God. Beyond reading about an ancient's worship experience, they need to worship.

Another implication of this principle is that Bible study doesn't take place within a capsule, sealed off from the rest of the learner's experience. When class members show up for Bible study, they don't come out of a vacuum. They bring leftover feelings from angry conflicts, gnawing pressures, and disappointed hopes; the satisfaction of achievements and the warm glow of affectionate relationships; the burden of unresolved decisions and anxieties over health problems and troubled family affairs. They don't check their lives at the door. Nor should they. Bible study at its best engages the whole life of the whole person.

3. *Goal-centered teaching is more efficient than teaching that has no particular purpose.*

In goal-centered teaching, lesson planning begins with the setting of definite goals. All the learning activities are designed to achieve those goals. "To present an overview of the Ten Commandments" is an aim which says nothing about learning goals. It merely says what the teacher plans to do;

it doesn't indicate what learners are expected to learn. In contrast, consider this goal: "By the end of this study, class members should be able to list and give a brief explanation of each of the Ten Commandments." That suggests goal-centered teaching.

Goal-centered teaching is more efficient. That is to say, it has the power to produce a desired result with the least amount of wasted effort and squandered resources.

I can illustrate this principle, in a negative sort of way. Come with me, if you will, to a men's Bible class in a large urban church which shall go unnamed. After ten minutes of idle chatter and record-taking, the teacher starts the lesson by asking everyone to turn to the second chapter of Ephesians. "Why don't we each read . . . let's see . . . about two verses each will divide it up fairly easily."

So we each read two verses. I can't listen to anyone else very carefully because I'm busy trying to figure out which two verses I'm supposed to read.

"Now," says the teacher, "what verses in this chapter strike you as really being important?"

No response.

"What about verses 8 and 9?" Everyone looks dutifully at verses 8 and 9. "This tells us that salvation is based on faith and not works, doesn't it?" Two or three men nod in agreement. "That was one of the first verses I ever memorized," the teacher continues. (Pause) "What else?"

No one knows for sure what the question means.

The teacher helps us out again. "Look at verse 13." He pauses while we look. "What does this tell us?" Then he answers his own question. "This verse tells us that we're saved by the blood of Christ. There's no other way."

He came close that time, I think to myself, *but that doesn't quite catch up the point.* Before I can decide whether or not to make an issue of it, the teacher jumps in again.

"Does anyone have any comments about another verse?"

There's no point in reproducing the dialogue for the rest of this session. Suffice it to say that it goes on like this for another fifteen minutes, then comes to an abrupt conclusion when the teacher announces, "Well, our time's about up. Remember to study your lesson for next Sunday. And let's all go to church today. Carl, lead us in prayer."

Here we have a clear illustration of "teaching" (if I may use the term broadly) which is definitely not goal-centered. It goes everywhere and nowhere at the same time. If "efficient" means, as my dictionary puts it, "producing a desired result," there's no way that this approach to Bible study can be called efficient. Unfortunately, it happens often. (The class session which we have just attended was real. Only a few details were changed to protect the innocent.)

4. *Learners are more likely to participate in learning activities when the teacher establishes an appropriate "set" at the beginning of the lesson.*

I have vowed to steer clear of educational jargon in this book. But "set" is a fairly useful term to describe what should happen at the beginning of a learning session. You can get a pretty good picture of its meaning if you'll think about what happens when someone starts a race by saying, "Ready? Get *set*. . . ." At this moment, all the runners tighten their muscles, prepare to spring into action, and tilt their bodies in the direction of the goal. Every distraction is forgotten as they concentrate with every fiber of their being on the race ahead.

Translate that into a teaching-learning situation. To establish "set" means to get the learners ready to plunge into learning activities, to tilt them toward the learning goal for the session, to rid them of distractions and competing influences. Put simply, to "establish set" is to cause the learners to want to study the lesson.

How do you do this? We will deal with this question in more detail in chapter 6; but I'll offer a few quick illustrations now, just to clarify the idea.

To establish set at the beginning of a lesson, you might:

• Ask a question designed to grip the imagination or tickle the curiosity of the learner. ("If you were given a million dollars, tax free, how would it change your life?" "Apart from the Bible, what is the most important book ever written?" "When a survey was taken among several thousand evangelical Christians, what do you suppose they chose as their most popular hymn?")

• Pose a hypothetical situation. "Imagine that you live in a country which has been occupied by enemy troops. Theirs is a cruel totalitarian government. Last night a high-ranking army officer was killed by a small band of men in your village who are generally regarded as hot-headed extremists. This is known among the people of your village, but the enemy troops have no idea who did the killing. Today, however, their commandment issued a shocking ultimatum. Unless the identity of the assassins is revealed, half of the people of the village—men, women, and children—will be machine-gunned in the square. Hastily, a few of the village leaders call a secret meeting. You are among them. What will you advise them to do?")

• Introduce conflicting ideas. ("Would you agree that one of the purposes of prayer is to let God know our needs? How, then, do you explain Matthew 6:8, RSV: 'Your Father knows what you need before you ask him'?")

• Tell a dramatic story. (An episode from the life of Corrie Ten Boom, for example.)

• Use a striking quotation. ("If you do not pray to God

daily, the reason is simple: You do not like God. And the sooner you face up to that truth, the better.")

5. *When a teacher uses questions, they should vary in form, scope, and level of difficulty.*

This principle is more specific than the others. But I wanted to include it as an example of the kind of teaching principle which has to do with methodology. (There are others, of course; and they will be dealt with in chapter 8.)

Question-asking is one of the most widely used of all teaching techniques. It is also widely misused. Consider the following questions, as they might be used to lead a class in a study of Abram's family heritage and his call in Genesis 11 and 12. "According to Genesis 11:26, who was Abram's father? Who were his brothers? Can you find the name of Abram's wife in this passage? Where did the family settle after they left Ur of the Chaldees?"

How do these questions strike you? Do they grab your interest? Challenge your intellect? Fill you with curiosity? I doubt it. What's wrong with them? They are simplistic. Mature learners would be bored by them. All you have to do to answer them is to look at the text and spot the right words. Most of us learned to do that in elementary school.

Questions which may be answered with a yes or no are also limited in learning potential. It doesn't require much thought to hazard a guess when you know you have a fifty-fifty chance to get it right. Here is an example of such a question: "Did Abram travel far after leaving Haran in response to God's command?" The question requires a minimum of information. Either Abram did travel far, or he didn't. If the answer isn't yes, it obviously is no. Another problem is the ambiguity of the question. How far is "far"?

Let's compare another "how-not-to-do-it" example with a "how-to-do-it" right" version. (Also based on Abram's story in the early verses of Gen. 12.) First: "Do you think that Abram found it difficult to leave Haran and go to an unknown country?" Again, we have a yes-no type of question. Learners can answer it off the top of their heads. But this next question gets at the same thing in a more thought-provoking way: "What personal, social, economic, and physical difficulties did Abram experience as a result of his decision to leave Haran?" Or, if you want to draw learners into it on a more personal level: "Had you been Abram, facing the decision to leave your home in Haran, what factors would have made it hard for you to leave?"

Teachers' questions also differ in terms of their scope. That is to say, some are narrow and some are broad. Narrow questions have only one possible answer; broad questions are open to several possibilities. Compare a simple game of hopscotch with a complex maze, such as the "glass-house" at a carnival. Hopscotch requires agility, but every player has to follow the same path. A complicated maze, on the other hand, offers alternative routes at many points. Narrow questions are like hopscotch; there's only one way to go. Broad questions are like a maze; they open up a number of possibilities.

Here is an example of a narrow question: "Name the Old Testament prophet who inherited Elijah's mantle." This permits only one correct answer. But consider this one: "What role did prophets play in the history of ancient Israel?" You can walk around in that maze for quite a while, and the hard thinking done in the process might be more important than the answers you finally write on the chalkboard.

The moral to all of this is not that you should always avoid simple or narrow questions. The point is that questions of this nature should not be used all of the time, or even most of the time. As a general rule, questions should be varied in form, scope, and level of difficulty.

TEACHING LAB ACTIVITY NO. 13

This activity will provide practice in rewriting questions. I will give questions which are too simple, too narrow, or written in yes-no form. Your job will be to come up with improved versions.

A. Rewrite the following yes-no question so as to make it more thought-provoking: "When God commanded Jonah to go to Nineveh (Jonah 1:1-3), was the prophet eager to go?

B. The next question calls for the recitation of a simple fact reported in the story of Jonah. Rewrite it so as to discover the reasons behind Jonah's attitude; make the learners use their reasoning ability. "When the people of Nineveh repented and were spared from God's judgment, what was Jonah's attitude?" (Jonah 3:6 to 4:1).

C. Here is an example of a narrow question: "What finally caused Pharaoh to let the Israelites leave Egypt?" (Ex. 12:29-33). Can you come up with a broader one, based on the same biblical episode?

D. Assuming that you are teaching a group of adult learners, what would be the main weakness of this question: "Where was Saul of Tarsus headed at the time of his conversion experience?" (Acts 9). Can you improve upon it?

Any of the questions above could have been rewritten in a dozen ways. So don't regard the following examples as the final word. I offer them simply to illustrate how each of the questions given earlier might be improved:

A. "When God commanded Jonah to go to Nineveh, *why* was the prophet reluctant to go?"

B. "When the people of Nineveh repented and were spared from God's judgment, *why* was Jonah disappointed and angry?"

C. "Why was Pharaoh reluctant to let the Israelites leave Egypt?"

D. "What do you suppose Saul of Tarsus would have done in Damascus had he not been converted?"

In the foregoing discussion, you looked briefly at five teaching principles. Can you remember them well enough to complete the following statements?

1. People will try harder to learn when the learning gives them _____, _____ _____, or promises to be _____.

2. In learning groups, the level of participation is higher when teaching activities are directed to _____ _____ _____.

108

3. _____-_____ teaching is more _____ than teaching that has no particular purpose in mind.

4. Learners are more likely to participate in learning activities when the teacher establishes an appropriate ___ at the beginning of the lesson.

5. When a teacher uses questions, they should _____ in _____, _____, and _____ _____ _____.

This, of course, is not a complete list of teaching principles; not by a long shot. These five principles were chosen simply to illustrate what we mean by "principles of teaching." You will find a lot more information about principles of teaching in later chapters.

Let's Review This Chapter

What does a Bible teacher need to know? There are many, many possible answers to a question like that. But, in this chapter, we've focused on three areas of knowledge: (1) knowledge of the Bible, (2) knowledge of learners, and (3) knowledge of teaching principles. Let me give you a sentence which, though clumsy gramatically, will help you to get these areas of knowledge fixed in your memory. Just remember the question:

WHAT is taught to WHOM, HOW?

With this formula in mind, fill in the blanks below:

1. A teacher needs a knowledge of (WHAT?) the _____.

2. A teacher needs a knowledge of (WHOM?) _____.

3. A teacher needs a knowledge of (HOW?) _____.

The teacher's biblical knowledge. It would be unrealistic to insist that every teacher be a walking encyclopedia of Bible knowledge. But every teacher should be a growing student of the Bible; for those who handle the sacred Word have an obligation to handle it rightly. Perversion of Scripture is even worse than ignorance of it. The best safeguard against perversion of biblical truth is diligent study bathed in an attitude of dependence upon the Holy Spirit. "If any of you lack wisdom, let him ask of God, that giveth to all men liberally, and upbraideth not; and it shall be given him" (Jas. 1:5).

The very nature of biblical revelation makes it essential for the interpreter to take into account the historical origin of the Scriptures. To do otherwise is to let revealed truth be displaced by imagined truth. The faithful student of the Bible will first try to determine what the writer was saying to his original readers in their own historical setting, then identify universal truths which go beyond that original setting, and, finally, answer the question, "What do these truths mean for me today?"

This means, among other things, that the teacher will make a serious attempt to understand the nature of each book of the Bible, since this provides a necessary background for the interpretation of specific passages. The teacher will also learn to use Bible study tools, especially those which enable us to "use the Bible to interpret the Bible."

The Bible teacher cannot be content to limit his or her Bible study to current lessons. In order to "teach out of the overflow," one must build up a reservoir of Bible knowledge. The best way to accomplish this is to follow a systematic plan of personal Bible study, one which goes beyond immediate lesson preparation.

The teacher's knowledge of learners. Teaching and learning, like selling and buying, is a two-sided transaction. The teacher can't afford to be indifferent to the nature of learners any more than the salesman can afford to be indifferent to the needs and interests of his customer. This is true for three reasons. First, the teacher does not know what she has taught until she knows what the learner has heard. The message is shaped by the learner's hearing of it as well as by the teacher's understanding of it. Second, the teacher must meet the learners in her class at their own level of understanding and interest. Third, the teacher must be sensitive to those places in the lives of learners where biblical revelation touches personal experience.

Bible teachers may develop a knowledge of learners on two levels, the general and the specific. On the general level, studies in human development can provide insights into the characteristics of particular age groups. On the specific level, the teacher seeks to know as much as possible about individual class members.

The teacher's knowledge of teaching. Just as every cook has a style all her own, so does every teacher. Yet, just as there are generally accepted rules for cooking, there are principles of teaching which have proven their worth as guidelines in teaching-learning situations. We looked at five typical examples to illustrate the nature of teaching principles. (Remember that many more principles of teaching will be treated in greater detail in the next five chapters.)

4
How to Study a Lesson

In the not-too-distant future you will walk into a room occupied by people who have gathered to study the Bible. They will look to you for leadership. What they learn will depend in large measure on how well you fulfill your role as teacher. The time has come to start making preparation for that hour. But where do you start? What do you do first? That's what we want to take up in this chapter.

In an earlier chapter we compared teaching with guiding a newcomer through a strange city. To be a dependable guide one needs to have a good working knowledge of the terrain he proposes to cover. And this applies to one who plans to guide others through the Bible. You must have a good working knowledge of the material you propose to cover. Before deciding how to teach the lesson, you will want to study the lesson.

Blessed Is the Early Starter

Only once in my life did I ever arrive at the airport too late to catch an airplane. It was Saturday morning, and I did some puttering around the house before leaving. Since packing isn't one of my favorite pastimes, I puttered before I packed. I was still puttering at 10:20 when I decided to call the airport, just to be sure my flight would be on time. "Yes, sir, Flight 469 will depart on schedule at 10:50," said a sweet voice on the other end of the line.

"Did you say 10:50?" I stammered. "I thought it left at

11:50!" "No, sir," the agent assured me, "Flight 469 is scheduled to depart at 10:50."

In a state of panic I dashed into the bedroom, plopped a suitcase onto the bed, and started throwing things at it. Seven minutes later I dashed out of the house and leaped into the car. *Eighteen minutes,* I thought, *that's what it'll take to get to the airport—if the traffic isn't heavy.* Fortunately, the Saturday morning traffic on the expressway was moderate but, unfortunately, I had to park the car a good distance from the terminal. I arrived at the ticket counter breathing hard and in a sweat. To my dismay, there were several people standing in line. But I finally got a ticket and sprinted down the concourse, bag in hand, arriving at the gate just in time to see my flight roll away.

As it turned out, it was just as well that I didn't catch that flight; for, returning home and repacking with greater care, I found that I had failed to put in a suit, extra trousers, shaver, and conference notes.

I blush to admit it, but there have been times when I have dashed into a Bible study session about as well-prepared to teach as I was to leave on that trip. Not very well packed. And the problem in both instances was that I had waited too late to start preparing. Having learned this lesson the hard way, I want to pass on some friendly advice. Start early, if you want to teach with greater confidence, more effectiveness, and fewer stomach ulcers.

There are several good reasons for getting an early start on lesson preparation:

First, few of us can do our best work under pressure. Yes, I know that the world is full of people who vow; "I work best under pressure." What they really mean, more often than not, is that the *only* time they buckle down to work is when they get under pressure.

In the hair-raising experience described earlier, I most

certainly proved that I don't do my best packing under pressure. And that's true of almost any task you can name. I don't rake leaves, paint a wall, type a letter, or prepare an income tax return very well when I'm in a hurry. Do you? And I certainly don't do my most creative Bible study that way. Under time pressures, I tend to leave references unchecked, parallel readings unread, and enrichment materials unused.

Second, we can't always estimate how much time the preparation of a lesson will require. If we start early, we leave ourselves a margin of time. If we start too late, we don't really finish the preparation; we just quit when time runs out.

Third, teachers who begin their preparation early can take advantage of enrichment resources that are denied to the tardy. Teaching materials often suggest excellent books, pamphlets, films, and other supplementary materials. When lesson preparation is postponed too long, however, there isn't enough time to order, borrow, or gather such materials.

Fourth, when we don't leave enough time for lesson preparation, we tend to fall back on teaching methods which require the least amount of preparation. It takes time to prepare for role play, case studies, panel discussions, inductive Bible study, and audiovisual presentations. When preparation time is lacking, such procedures will go unused, and teaching will continue in the same, familiar pattern; not because the familiar pattern is better, but because it is easier.

Fifth, creative teaching requires time. Our best ideas come when our thinking has had time to "simmer" a while. It's like cooking a good meat sauce for Italian spaghetti. You can turn out a mundane dish in an hour; but if you want your spaghetti sauce to be in the gourmet class, it takes longer. So it is with teaching.

Some will say, "I stay so busy; I just can't seem to get

started on the lesson early." But, being busy is a very good argument for starting early. In the long run, an early beginning actually saves time. Why? Because it enables you to use remnants of time which you would otherwise squander.

That's the key to finding enough time to study your lesson. Use those scraps of time which turn up at odd moments. Work on a lesson after you send the children off to school and sit down for a second cup of coffee; or while you wait to pick them up after school. Grab some study time while you wait for your car pool or during those extra minutes on your lunch hour.

One of my friends is a used-car sales manager whose job requires him to be at the office early, usually half-an-hour before anyone else arrives. So he gets things opened up each morning, then spends thirty minutes studying his Bible. It doesn't seem like much, at first glance, but that's two-and-a-half hours of study per week, in time which might otherwise be wasted.

My wife and I both teach Bible classes, and we like to talk about upcoming lessons at breakfast. On Monday morning we read the Bible passage which we will be teaching the following Sunday. This precipitates a conversation which we hate to break off when time runs out. As a matter of fact, we don't break it off. We continue that conversation all week, saving up a valuable fund of ideas.

Getting into a lesson several days early keeps you thinking about it; and this thinking has a cumulative effect. You'll pick up ideas as you go along. For example, I had been pondering a lesson about Abram's call and departure from his home in Haran (Gen. 12:1 ff.) for several days when I spotted a newspaper article about a boat crowded with Vietnamese refugees lying off the coast of Malaysia. They had not been permitted to land there and were, quite literally, people without a country. "Hey," I said, "that would make a great illustration for the lesson on Abram. He must have felt a lot like those people when he pulled up his roots and left his homeland for a country that he had yet to see."

Then, only a day or two later, I was typing some of the material in chapter 3 of this book, and it struck me that Abram's experience had a great deal of relevance to vocational crises in middle adulthood. It's so hard to turn loose of the things that provide security; so difficult to launch out in new directions. But Abram did just that; and he was no young pup when he left the security of Haran.

Both of these illustrations just fell into my lap, so to speak. I hadn't wasted any time searching for them. And neither of them would have caught my attention had I not started thinking about this lesson well in advance.

Tools of the Trade

Before we get into the actual preparation of the lesson, let's think about some of the tools that you will need for the task.

A copy of the textbook, of course. Bible study is just that—*Bible* study. The Bible is the textbook. Everything else is supplementary. So, naturally, your copy of the Scriptures is the most essential ingredient in lesson preparation.

Ideally, you ought to have more than one copy of the Bible at your disposal. For one thing, you should read more than one English version. Why? Because you'll often gain an insight from one version which you might not pick up from another version. For example, compare Romans 8:28 in two different versions. The King James Version says: "And we know that all things work together for good to them that love God. . . ." But the Revised Standard Version says: "We know that in everything God works for good with those who love him. . . ." Notice that in the RSV the primary actor (the subject of the verb "works") is "God," rather than "things." And that makes a tremendous difference in meaning. Am I trying to say that the RSV is superior in every instance to the KJV? No, not at all. The point is that if you will compare different versions of the passage which you are studying, you will pick up small differences in interpretation.

Does that sound expensive, having more than one version of the Bible? Not necessarily. You can pick up surprisingly inexpensive editions of the Scriptures in modern language versions. The *Good News Bible,* one of the best, is also one of the least expensive. You can buy a copy for less than it costs to buy a small beef roast for your Sunday dinner.

Different Bibles have different purposes. By all means, get yourself a good reference Bible, with center-column references and interpretive notes. The *Oxford Annotated Bible* is a good example. And many people enjoy using the *Thompson Chain-Reference Bible.* But you'll also need a Bible which you don't mind marking up as you study; one with wide enough margins to leave room for your notes.

Bible study helps. So many Bible study helps are available today, it would be impossible to buy or use them all. But I want to suggest four Bible study tools which are basic, even essential—a concordance, a Bible dictionary, a Bible atlas, and Bible commentaries.

The uses of a concordance were outlined in chapter 3, and it will hardly be necessary to cover that ground again. Suffice it to say that the student of the Bible should no more think about being without a concordance than a carpenter would consider working without a saw. A concordance opens up a storehouse of information which would otherwise be difficult to acquire. And this valuable tool need not be expensive. Though you can spend several dollars on some concordances, you can also buy paperbound editions at relatively low cost.

Bible dictionaries also vary widely in quality, size, and price. Multivolume dictionaries, such as the *Interpreter's Dictionary of the Bible,* call for a fairly large investment of funds. When you consider the fact that this is a lifetime investment, though, the cost doesn't seem so great. On the other hand, there are several inexpensive one-volume dictionaries on the market. A Bible dictionary is an invaluable source of information on names, places, events, objects, and concepts found in the Scriptures.

If you want to see how far Abram traveled from Haran to the Negeb, or locate Mount Sinai where Moses received the Ten Commandments, or trace Paul's missionary journeys, a Bible atlas is the answer. Bible atlases have maps covering all the lands of the Bible in every period of biblical history. Some include comments on the geography and history of Bible lands. Many editions of the Bible contain maps, of course. But a Bible atlas offers two distinct advantages. Its maps are usually larger and more detailed; and it can free you from the bothersome necessity of flipping the pages of your Bible from text to the map section. As in the case of concordances and Bible dictionaries, some very good Bible atlases may be obtained in inexpensive paperbound editions.

The selection of Bible commentaries is much more complicated. They come in such endless variety. One writer estimated that no less than 600 commentaries had been written on the book of Psalms alone. Commentaries vary greatly in size, weight, theological perspective, quality, and cost. The other day, I came across a new commentary on the Gospel of Luke; the "prepublication discount price" was thirty-two dollars! On the other hand, one of my most valued commentaries on Romans cost only ninety-five cents.

Bible commentaries provide a rich treasury of interpretations and insights into biblical knowledge, and they should hold a significant place in the Bible teacher's kit of Bible study tools.

Consider the possibility of buying single volumes on the respective books of the Bible as you need them. (Remember that volumes in sets may also be purchased separately.) A ten-dollar commentary on the Gospel of John isn't an unreasonable investment for, say, a three-month study, especially when you consider the fact that this will be a permanent addition to your shelf of Bible study resources. (Commentaries seldom become outdated. Many good ones were written more than fifty years ago, and some have been around for centuries.) Purchase one commentary periodically and you'll be surprised at how quickly your collection can grow.

A ten-dollar commentary is too rich for your budget? That need not stop you. Many Bible commentaries, even some of the best ones, are available in inexpensive editions. Low cost shouldn't be one's sole reason for selecting a commentary; but that isn't sufficient reason for rejecting one, either. Many a masterpiece of interpretation may be found in a plain binding.

One-volume commentaries on the whole Bible can provide a lot of help at comparatively low cost. The chief disadvantage of these is that they cover a lot of territory in a limited number of pages; and this means that interpretations of specific passages can't be covered in much detail.

With such a variety of commentaries available, how does one go about selecting the right ones? The best approach is to seek the advice of someone you respect—a pastor, teacher, or book store salesperson—and whose doctrinal views are generally compatible with yours. And if you are fortunate enough to have a good church library at your disposal, don't fail to take advantage of it.

Church curriculum materials. If you are teaching the Bible in a church context, you probably use curriculum materials (sometimes called "Sunday School quarterlies"). These offer important advantages. First, they provide some assurance that the Church's Bible study program won't go galloping off in all directions. A church is obligated to monitor the doctrinal content of Bible lessons. In the New Testament, we find a number of passages containing warnings against teaching or tolerating false doctrine (Gal. 1:6-9; Eph. 4:14; 2 Tim. 1:13-14; 2:14-17; Titus 2:1; Rev. 2:14-16). While a church-adopted curriculum provides no ironclad guarantee against false teaching, it does prescribe basic boundaries. Second, a standardized curriculum will provide a common pool of ideas for teachers and learners in the Bible study experience. Third, most curricula are planned so as to provide balanced coverage of the Scriptures over extended periods. Any Bible study group could plan such an agenda, of course; but more often than not, classes which use no curriculum material for guidance tend to favor some portions of the Bible, and neglect others.

As useful as curriculum materials are, they should be kept in proper perspective. A lesson periodical is, like the other resources discussed earlier, an aid to Bible study. It is not the textbook for the class—the Bible is. It is not the final word on interpretation, not the only source of information for teachers and learners. The teacher who studies only a lesson periodical, ignoring even the text of the Bible itself, is literally "eccentric" ("off-center") in lesson preparation.

Look Around Before You Dig

I was short on money and long on ambition. So I decided to install my own chain-link fence. Though a rank amateur at that sort of thing, I knew enough not to march out into my back yard and start digging a posthole. No, I looked around first. It wasn't enough just to decide on a starting place; I also had to know where the fence would end, and what obstructions it might encounter. I measured carefully; laboriously. Then I started digging the first posthole.

One's approach to a Bible lesson ought to follow a similar pattern. You don't just turn to a selected Bible passage and start digging in; not before "surveying the terrain" around it. "What comes before and what comes after this particular passage?" "What is the nature of the book of the Bible in which it appears?" "Who is the author, who is the audience, and what are the main issues in this book?" "How does this lesson fit in with the lessons which precede and follow it?" Such questions need answering before you focus on the lesson itself.

Obviously, you won't have to cover this ground each time you sit down to study a lesson. You do this "backgrounding" only as you begin a study in a new book of the Bible.

The first step is to become familiar with the general nature of the portion of the Bible which you are going to study. At the beginning of a series on Old Testament prophecy, read an article on prophecy in a Bible dictionary or encyclopedia.

Before you start a twelve-week study of some book of the Bible, read an introduction to that book in a commentary or Bible encyclopedia. Find an outline of the book (most commentaries have them) and get an overview of its content.

The second step is to scan the material for the next several lessons, to see how they fit together. Don't think in terms of individual lessons. Think in terms of units of study. In a curriculum periodical, the material will be broken into units already, the specific number of lessons in a unit being determined by the natural divisions in the biblical material.

If you are not using a lesson periodical, create your own units. Arrange the material in blocks of several lessons. Some like to proceed chapter by chapter, one chapter per session. But this isn't always a good idea, because it doesn't take into account the variety in biblical material. It is doubtful that your class would want to devote a whole session to the long genealogy in Genesis 10. But you could profitably spend a whole session on *each* of the Ten Commandments in Exodus 20. And you certainly couldn't deal adequately with the Beatitudes (Matt. 5:1-12) in a single session. The best approach is to let the material outline itself, taking into consideration the amount of time needed to cover each portion of Scripture.

Let me suggest a specific routine for previewing the lessons in an upcoming unit of study. Start by listing all of the Scripture passages to be studied. Then read through these passages, preferably in a modern English version. This will provide an overview of the material and help you to see how the passages fit together. If you use a curriculum periodical, read the introduction to the unit.

Next, go back over the lessons one by one. Don't attempt to study them in detail at this point; but try to answer these questions about each lesson:

• What is the main emphasis, the central idea, in this passage of Scripture?

• What other ideas will be of interest to my class?

• What can my class members gain from this lesson, in terms of their personal needs and interests? In other words, why should they study this particular lesson?

• What will I need to give particular attention to as I study this lesson further?

I strongly recommend keeping a notebook with one page devoted to each lesson. Begin each page with an identifying title for the lesson, the date on which it is to be taught, and the Scripture passage to be covered. Then jot down answers to the questions above.

The following example illustrates what I have in mind:

TITLE: The Word Became Flesh
DATE: December 16
SCRIPTURE: John 1:1-18
CENTRAL IDEA: The eternal Word makes his dwelling place among men.
OTHER IDEAS: (1) The eternal nature of Christ and his role in creation. (2) Christ as the source of life and light. (3) The obligation of those who have seen the light to bear witness to it, as exemplified by John.
WHAT CLASS MEMBERS CAN GAIN FROM THIS LESSON: A great lesson on evangelism. Verse 12, especially, should speak to non-Christians in our class. And the lesson should challenge those who are Christians to be witnesses.
FURTHER STUDY: (1) This concept of the Logos, the Word, seems to have special significance to John. I'll need to look into this. (2) Is the Word different from, or same as, God? Verses 1 and 2 seem to imply both. (3) An article on "incarnation" in a Bible encyclopedia would help.

This notebook can serve as a useful depository of notes, illustrative material, and teaching ideas for each lesson. It's nice to have such a head start when you sit down to prepare a specific lesson.

Before we go on to other things, why don't you try your hand at writing down preliminary notes on a lesson? The following teaching lab activity will give you some practice:

TEACHING LAB ACTIVITY NO. 14

Instructions: In this exercise you will be processing a Scripture passage. Assume that it is included in a unit of study which you soon will teach. Use a Bible passage of your own choosing. If you are presently teaching, select a passage from a future unit of study. If you have nothing else in mind, use Luke 10:29-37 for this exercise.

First, read the passage. Think about its relationship to the class which you are teaching or the class which you attend. Then jot down your responses to the questions below.

LESSON TITLE:

DATE ON WHICH IT WILL BE TAUGHT:

SCRIPTURE:

WHAT IS THE MAIN EMPHASIS OR CENTRAL IDEA?

ARE THERE OTHER IDEAS THAT WOULD INTEREST THE CLASS?

WHAT CAN MEMBERS OF YOUR CLASS GAIN FROM THIS LESSON?

WHAT NEEDS SPECIAL ATTENTION AS YOU DO
FURTHER STUDY?

===

Studying the Lesson

We finally come to the subject promised in the title of
this chapter. But, of course, we have been dealing with this
subject all along. For these are quite essential preliminaries.
To avoid them is to short-circuit the process of lesson preparation. It's like telling someone how to plant a garden. You
must talk about preparing the soil before you talk about
putting the seed into the ground.

But let's get down to specifics. Assuming that the ground-
work has been completed, how do you study a lesson?

Read the passage devotionally. Let the lesson passage
speak to your heart as well as to your head as you read
through it initially. Bathe your reading in prayer. Let the
Spirit "guide you into all truth." Be open to whatever God
will reveal to you. Do this first reading of the passage early;
and do it more than once. Use different versions of the Bible,
if possible.

Read the passage analytically. Go through the passage
again; but, this time, with an eye for detail. Here are some
ways to pull meaning out of the passage:

1. As you read, use your pencil freely. Mark unfamiliar
words. Underline key phrases. Use exclamation marks in
the margins to identify important ideas; use question marks
to identify anything which raises questions. Write notes to
yourself for later reference.

2. Look up parallel passages listed in the center-column or marginal references. This will take a little time; but it will pay rich dividends in added insight and understanding.

3. Ask yourself questions about the passage: What was said to whom? For what purpose? With what result? What does it mean?

At this point in the process, a teacher's notations on Hebrews 4:11-13 might look something like this:

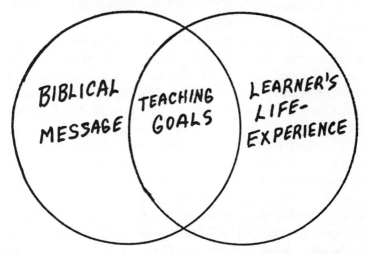

Use Bible study tools. Remember those Bible study helps described earlier? Concordances, dictionaries, atlases, and commentaries? This is the time to use them in your study. Here are some things you can do with them:

1. Look up the meanings of key words in a Bible dictionary and use a concordance to see how they are used in other Bible passages. Key words often appear several times in a passage, or in a book of the Bible. "Blessed," in the Beatitudes Matt. 5:3-11, is an example. "Word," in John 1:1-18,

and "love," in 1 Corinthians 13, are key words. The word *rest* holds a similarly important position in Hebrews 3 and 4.

A Bible dictionary will give you information about the biblical meanings of such words, just as an English dictionary will give you word meanings. And don't assume that you are familiar with the biblical meanings simply because the words are commonly used in the English language. Such words as "heart," "soul," "love," and "holy" can have very unique meanings in Scripture.

One way to understand key words is to see how they are used in other portions of the Bible. Look at the parallel uses of "word" and "word of God" in the example based on Hebrews 4:11-13 which you looked at earlier. These additional uses of key words may be located with the help of a concordance.

2. Look up the names of any persons or places with which you are unfamiliar. A Bible dictionary will be a good source of information. But a concordance will give you some help here, too. Let's say, for example, that you come across the name, Melchizedek, in Hebrews 7:1, for the first time. A concordance reveals that Melchizedek also appears in Genesis 14:18, the historical point of reference for the writer's argument in Hebrews 7. (The same information may also be found in a center-column reference.)

3. Use a Bible atlas to look up locations of places mentioned in the passage. Such information is often of more than passing interest. For instance, the great distance traversed by Abram in his journey from Haran to the Negeb says much about the magnitude of his faith. A short jaunt from Haran to Hamath would have been less impressive. And a glance at a map will help the reader of John 11 appreciate the reluctance of Jesus' disciples (v. 8) and the courage

of Thomas (v. 16), when the Master announced his decision to go to Bethany after the death of Lazarus. For Bethany is close to Jerusalem, where, not long before, the Jews had tried to stone Jesus to death (10:31-39).

4. Consult commentaries for interpretations of the passage. Bible commentaries contain a wealth of factual information and intriguing interpretations of Scripture. So long as the reader keeps firmly in mind the differences between facts and subjective interpretations, commentaries can provide invaluable assistance. We should approach Bible commentaries with healthy appreciation for the dedicated scholarship of those who write them; but this should be counter-balanced by an equally healthy realization that no interpretation is sacred simply because it appears on the printed page. Where commentators tend to agree, we can accept their conclusions with a reasonable degree of confidence. Where they differ, we must weigh the evidence and draw our conclusions in the light of our best understandings. And where it is impossible to come to a conclusion, we should have the humility to acknowledge this. Teachers of the Bible should never be embarrassed to say "I'm not sure." They are in a lot of good company, including even those who think they are sure.

This word of caution against accepting a commentator's interpretation lock, stock, and barrel, applies as well to Sunday School lesson commentaries. These appear in great number on the shelves of religious bookstores and in the mail-order catalogs of religious publishing houses. And some of them enjoy tremendous popularity with teachers. Obviously, they are useful. But their very usefulness causes them to be misused.

Let me be frank. I'm talking about teachers who buy their favorite lesson commentary each year, consult no other source during lesson preparation, and, taking their commentaries to class, teach(?) the lesson straight from its pages, reading choice quotations (previously underlined) as they go along. Such complete dependence upon a single source of interpretation is, in reality, a subtle subordination of biblical truth to the views of a single individual, the writer of the commentary.

Consult curriculum materials. In all candor, it should be said that teachers can become as dependent upon "teachers' quarterlies" as they can upon lesson commentaries. It is no more desirable to teach the lesson straight from the pages of a teacher's periodical than it is to lecture from any other lesson commentary. To teachers of the Bible, "studying the lesson" should mean something more than reading a few pages in a curriculum piece.

But curriculum materials are an important adjunct to lesson preparation, especially since they are used to guide the thinking of members in their own lesson preparation. That's why the teacher's initial study of the Bible passage should be supplemented by the lesson writer's interpretation. In many cases, you'll be getting more than a lesson writer's insights; for such curriculum materials are often the product of a team effort combining the resources of editors, writers, subject-matter experts, educators, and production specialists.

Compare the curriculum writer's views to your own findings up to this point. What are the similarities and differences in your interpretations? Has the curriculum writer emphasized points which had not occurred to you? Include these in your notes.

Pull it all together. If you have followed the procedures suggested thus far, you will have picked up ideas, information, and biblical interpretations from several different sources. No doubt, these will have produced a collection of written notes. But now it's time to process these raw materials.

Unfortunately, some teachers don't get around to processing the fruits of their initial study. They'll simply take into class the random notes they have made at the study desk. These notes might look something like this:

TITLE: "No Greater Love"
SCRIPTURE: 1 Corinthians 13

• Henry Drummond wrote a book in which he called love "the greatest thing in the world."

• This chapter on love is in the middle of a discussion of worship practices; especially the place of spiritual gifts in worship.

• Three words for love in the N. T.—*eros* (romantic love), *philia* (brotherly love, friendship), and *agape* (Christian love). Paul is talking about *agape* here. (One commentary says that these distinctions between the words for love aren't always clear.)

• Paul gets down to the nitty-gritty in verses 4-7 and lists practical characteristics of love:

"longsuffering" (patient)
"kind" (tries to be constructive)
"not envious" (not jealous)
"not puffed up" (not boastful; humble)
"doesn't behave unseemly" (not arrogant or rude)
"seeks not her own" (doesn't have to have own way)
"not easily provoked" (not irritable)
"thinks no evil" (not resentful)
"rejoices not in iniquity" (not resentful; doesn't keep an account of wrongs)
"rejoices in the truth" (is glad when right prevails)

"bears all things" (no limit to its endurance)

"believes all things" (is trusting)

"endures all things" (love can outlast anything)

(Note: Make application to family life, business, school, etc.)

• Jesus' disciples commanded to love one another—John 13:34.

• Love comes from God—Romans 5:5.

• The cross of Christ is supreme example of love—1 John 4:10.

• Love will outlast faith and hope, because when we see fully, we will no longer need faith, and when our hopes are fulfilled, we won't need hope; but love will be the rule by which we will all live in our eternal home.

• The lesson writer says that *eros* is an emotional response; but *agape* is something you *will* to do, even if the person loved is not lovable.

Such notes are like stacks of materials—lumber, bricks, concrete blocks—standing on a construction site before the builders arrive. They have potential, but they need to be pulled together into a coherent design. A good step in this direction is to identify the major ideas in the lesson. What makes an idea "major"? Two things, really. The writer's purpose and the relationship of the passage to the needs of your class.

Discerning the writer's purpose is of paramount importance, for this is the only way to be true to Scripture. Let me refer to a familiar passage to illustrate what I mean. Take a look at Philippians 2:4-11. Suppose I were to tell you that the main idea in this passage is the glorification of Christ at his second coming, and point to verses 9-11 in support of that contention. That would be a distortion of

Paul's intention in this passage; for his main emphasis here is not on the exaltation of Christ, but, quite to the contrary, on his self-imposed humiliation. Verses 1-5 hold the key to Paul's meaning. His argument runs something like this: "Relate to one another (as fellow Christians) in harmony and love. Don't be ruled by selfishness, but, rather, by humility. Don't be more concerned for yourself than you are for others. Just look at the example Christ gave us; he gave up his heavenly glory for a cross. That's the kind of self-giving spirit we ought to have toward one another."

To take another example, suppose I am preparing to lead a study of the twenty-third chapter of Matthew, and spotting verse 23, say to myself: "This will be an excellent opportunity to stress the importance of tithing." Now, it so happens that I am firmly committed to the practice of tithing as a tangible expression of my responsibility as a Christian steward. But I can't claim tithing is a major idea in this chapter without seriously twisting the meaning of Jesus' teaching here. In this passage, Jesus is speaking against a narrow-minded, nit-picking legalism which blinds one to the things that really matter. The things that really matter include justice, and mercy, and faith. And in verse 23 the meticulous tithing of small herbs and spices is actually presented in contrast to these "weightier matters." So, if I were to pretend that tithing is the major idea of the passage (or even *a* major idea), I would be perilously close to making the Bible say what I want it to say.

But remember, when attempting to identify the major ideas in a lesson passage, to keep the needs and interests of class members in focus. While you would not want to turn the meaning of a passage upside-down in order to make it fit the current needs of members, if a passage has more than one focal point, you certainly would want to select the emphases which speak most significantly to learners.

Think back, for a moment, to 1 Corinthians 13. Paul is discussing the appropriate uses of spiritual gifts in Christian worship; and he seems to be saying that love is both the greatest gift and the motive which should control the use of all other gifts. The discussion in 1 Corinthians 13 seems to be designed to support that point. But it is also designed to answer the questions, "What is love? How does it actually manifest itself in Christian relationships?" So, here we have two major ideas. First, how is love related to gifts of the Spirit? Second, what does it look like in actual operation? If your class members have been filled with questions about spiritual gifts, recently, you might want to focus on the first question. If the crying need of your members is to learn how to be more loving in relationships, on the other hand, the second question might assume greater importance.

Make no mistake about it. What we are talking about here is one of the more difficult steps in lesson preparation. Digging out information and putting it down on paper is time-consuming, but not so demanding. Deciding what to do with it is the hard part. For this reason, a little practice might be in order at this point. In the following teaching lab activity I want to give you a list of random information on each of three different Bible passages. This information is like the material which you might come up with in your initial exploration of the passages, with the help of concordances, atlases, dictionaries, and commentaries. Your job will be to identify the major ideas, those points which would form the best bases for lessons in your Bible class.

TEACHING LAB ACTIVITY NO. 15

Instructions: Below you will see a set of notes on each of three different Bible passages. Look over each set of notes, then select the *one* major idea in each passage which would serve as the best focal point for a lesson in your Bible class. Remember the two criteria for making your selections: (1) What was the writer's guiding purpose? (2) Where does this passage touch the needs and interests of the people in my class?

EXODUS 32

• The events in this passage came to pass while Moses was on Mount Sinai for a long time (v. 1; 24:18). People can't tolerate a leadership vacuum. In the absence of Moses, they "drafted" Aaron.

• They willingly gave up their gold earrings to make the golden calf (v. 3). Money and other resources are neutral; they can be used for good or evil.

• Aaron tried to compromise. He tried to include the real God (Yahweh) in the golden calf worship (v. 5). But this didn't work; the occasion turned into an orgy anyway (v. 6). You can't compromise in the worship of the living God. To try to worship him and other gods at the same time completely corrupts worship.

• King Jeroboam placed calves of gold at shrines in Bethel and Dan (1 Kings 12:28-29), in another instance of false worship.

• The "worship" experience of the people certainly wasn't one of reverence or consecration to God. After offering sacrifices they immediately "sat down to eat and drink," then "rose up to play" (a sexual orgy, the commentary says). Are we too concerned about entertainment, and not concerned enough about communing with God, in worship?

• The golden calf could have been either solid gold or a gold-plated wood carving.

• One commentator says that the fashioning of a calf might not have been a deliberate denial of the true God; it could have been an Israelite symbol for divine strength. But this still would have been a violation of one of the very Commandments given to Moses on Mount Sinai (Ex. 20:4).

• Sin so often rears its head even on sacred occasions. Even as Moses was receiving the law, the people were sinning against God. (Satan also got into the act at the Last Supper—John 13:27.)

• The people worshiped the wrong God, under the wrong leader, at the wrong altar, in the wrong way.

JOHN 2:12-25

• Jesus' cleansing of the Temple was more than an effort to reform or "clean up" temple worship. It was a sign of the Messiah's coming. (See Mal. 3:1 ff; Zech. 14:21.)

• The changing of money and selling of animals for sacrifice was part of a lucrative enterprise operated by the high priest and his family. No wonder they became so angry at Jesus!

• This was the first of three Passover feasts (v. 13) mentioned in the Gospel of John (see 6:4; 13:1). If Jesus' ministry lasted over three Passovers, this suggests that it lasted longer than two years but less than three.

• Pilgrims to Jerusalem had to buy oxen, sheep, and pigeons for the ritual of purification. And they had to have Jewish coinage to pay the half-shekel Temple tax. In Mark 11:17 Jesus denounces the dishonesty of the traders; but in this passage he denounces the whole business.

• There's always someone around to make a profit off of worship.

• In verse 19, Jesus was probably saying, "Go on as you are now doing and the Romans will destroy the Temple, but I will raise up another center of worship in three days [from his death to his resurrection]."

• Verse 20 contains a very accurate statement. Herod the Great started rebuilding the Temple in 20-19 B.C. Forty-six years from that date would place the events reported by John in A.D. 27 or 28.

• Jesus was perceptive enough to see that the faith of those who believed because of his miracles was shallow, so he didn't trust himself to them (vv. 23-25). It's the same today. People "believe" at many different levels of faith, and for many different reasons. Some have to see miracles (such as faith-healing). Some are "fair-weather" believers, forsaking Jesus (John 6:66-67) when the going gets tough.

GENESIS 11:1-9

• Babel probably means Babylon. Shinar is a Hebrew word which means the same thing as the Accadian word *Sumer,* which is the region lying to the south of Babylon.

• Nabopolassar, king of Babylon (625-605 B.C.) described restoration work which he carried out on the tower ("ziggurat") named Etemenanki. He says that he was commanded by the diety Marduk to "make its foundations secure in the nether world and make its summit like the heavens." He also mentions the materials described in Genesis 11:3, bricks and bitumen.

• The ziggurats of Mesopotamia were pyramid-like towers which had religious significance.

• God is not even mentioned in the planning of the tower spoken of in Genesis 11:4. These people wanted to "make a name for themselves." Their project was literally, god-less.

• The pride and self-sufficiency implied by verse 4 remind us of the serpent's words in Genesis 3:5, "ye shall be as gods." This is the real answer to the question, "What was wrong with what they did?"

• There is an almost humorous irony in verse 5. What these people thought was so tall, God had to *come down* to see.

• This is a classic example of the attitude and error of theological man. It is an attitude of self-sufficiency which does not need God, as reflected by the biochemist who said, "We have discovered the molecular structure of God." There is nothing wrong with technological progress; what is wrong is man's dependence upon his own ingenuity, rather than upon God.

• But don't we "build our cities and towers" in a variety of ways? Don't we depend upon insurance, bank accounts, retirement programs, and accumulations of material possessions for security, rather than depending upon God?

Earlier, we looked at some study procedures which should yield a collection of notes on significant words, names, places, parallel references, and interpretations of a lesson passage. Then I suggested that a first step toward pulling these together into an orderly arrangement would be to identify the major ideas in the passage. You have just completed a teaching lab activity designed to provide some practice in this. In the teaching lab exercise, you were asked to identify only one major idea in each passage. However, this will not always be the case. Sometimes you might even include three or four major ideas in a lesson, especially if one of the major ideas is broad enough to catch up several other points in the lesson. I want to present an example of that right now.

Let's say that you are preparing to teach a lesson based

on Genesis 12 and 13. These two chapters describe the travels of Abram after he leaves Haran in response to the command of God (12:1). As you study them, you can accumulate extensive notes, for these chapters are rich in place-names, personal names, and historical detail. They contain extraordinary ethical and theological insights. And they present a parade of historical events. It's very difficult to know what major ideas to single out.

But, as you study, you notice that Abram repeats one act over and over again. In Genesis 12:7 you read, "and there builded he an altar unto the Lord." And just below, in verse 8, "and there he builded an altar unto the Lord, and called upon the name of the Lord." Then again, in 13:4, he came back "unto the place of the altar, which he had made there at the first: and there Abram called on the name of the Lord." And after his separation from Lot, who "pitched his tent toward Sodom," Abram "removed his tent, and came and dwelt in the plain of Mamre, which is in Hebron, and built there an altar unto the Lord (13:18).

The altars of Abram are not just incidental details in a historical chronicle. They symbolize a deeply significant truth about the life of this ancient patriarch. He was a man of faith who lived in continual communion with God. To him, worship was as natural—and as essential—as eating and sleeping. It's a big idea; big enough to accommodate a number of auxiliary ideas. Let me illustrate:

(1) When Abram left Haran, he gave up those things in which most men find personal security; his home, his friends, the environment to which he was accustomed. But he left with the knowledge that he could never go beyond the greatest security a man can have, a knowledge of the living God, as symbolized by the altars he built.

(2) On the negative side, the only place where Abram

did not build an altar was in Egypt, where he seems to have undergone a period of moral and spiritual decline.

(3) But, after this lapse, Abram "went back to Bethel" where he renewed his vows to God at the altar which he had built previously. The altar was the same, but the man was changed.

(4) When Lot and his uncle came to a parting of the ways, Lot saw things through the eyes of a materialist, and made his choice accordingly. But Abram made his choice through the eyes of faith, foregoing immediate advantages in order to claim the ultimate promise. Lot had his fertile valley; but Abram had his altar.

This example illustrates an important principle about organizing the fruits of one's study. When you are able to identify a powerful idea, the material tends to fall into place around the idea. The idea becomes an organizing principle, bringing order and meaning to the rest of the data, much as a magnet held under a sheet of paper can bring scattered iron filings into an orderly arrangement.

In the book of Hosea, for instance, a strong organizing concept is the seemingly paradoxical emphasis on judgment and mercy, on the wrath of God and the love of God. Though poles apart in meaning, judgment and mercy appear in Hosea again and again, like two sides of a coin. When we start with this organizing concept, so much of the material in this Old Testament prophecy falls into a meaningful pattern. Read Hosea 1:6, then 1:7. See the contrasting themes? Then read verses 9 and 10 in the same way. There it is again. Chapter 2 offers another example. Note the contrast between the tone of verses 9-13 and verses 14-23. But the most beautiful example of this overarching concept is in Hosea 11. Notice how these two forces in the character of God, wrath and love, seem to be arguing with one another.

The Other Teacher at Your Study Desk

To talk about the teacher's personal lesson preparation without reference to the role of the Holy Spirit would be a serious omission. For the Spirit is the teacher's Teacher, illuminating the mind, warming the heart, and providing spiritual insight. As leaders of Bible study, we are "taught by the Spirit, interpreting spiritual truths to those who possess the Spirit" (1 Cor. 2:13, RSV).

As Jesus stood in the shadow of the cross, soon to be separated from his disciples, he spoke of the work of this other Teacher. "When the Spirit of truth comes," he said, "he will guide you into all truth; for he will not speak on his own authority, but whatever he hears he will speak, and he will declare to you the things that are to come" (John 16:13, RSV). Those disciples lived to see the fulfillment of that promise. The Spirit came in power, guiding the young churches, directing the missionary enterprise, and illuminating the minds of those who were commissioned to preach and teach the Word of God. And he continues to work among God's people today.

As you sit at your study desk, pondering the meaning of the Scriptures, the same Spirit who inspired the writers of that sacred Word is there to guide your interpretation of it. The Bible's message is a living Word precisely because it is revealed to us by the living Spirit. Biblical revelation is rooted in the pages of Scripture, but it is something more than the printed page. Biblical revelation is that which the Spirit brings to mind as you and I study the written word.

My mother, a teacher of women's Bible classes for many years, died of cancer after a six-month struggle with the disease. After her death, we found in her personal study Bible a living chronicle of her pilgrimage through those difficult days. We could tell which Scriptures she had been reading just before her final hospitalization; for her strength had wasted away, and the firm, bold handwriting with which she had always made notes in her Bible, finally turned into a feeble wavering scrawl. One day, only a short while before her death, she had drawn a faint line under the words in 1 Peter 5:7, "Casting all your care upon him; for he careth for you." It was a familiar verse. I had read it many times. Yet, I know that God spoke to her in a unique way on that occasion, and that those familiar words glowed with a meaning that was directed especially to his suffering child. The biblical revelation had become something more than the printed page.

One may read the words of Scripture without understanding, just as certain people listened to Jesus without really hearing. Commenting on their spiritual blindness, Jesus said, "Seeing they do not see, and hearing they do not hear, nor do they understand" (Matt. 13:13, RSV). But, turning to his disciples he said, "To you it has been given to know the secrets of the kingdom of heaven" (Matt. 13:11, RSV). And this is his promise to those who open themselves to the guidance of the Spirit at the study desk.

Time to Summarize Again

Do summaries at the ends of chapters bore you as much as they do me? I find it pretty easy to skip over them. "After all," I tell myself, "you've already been over the material once." Yet, I must confess that I don't always remember everything I have read in a chapter. And that's my main excuse for including them in these pages. For review. If you have missed something along the way, you'll be reminded; if you haven't, a brief review will help to reinforce what you have picked up along the way.

This chapter, you will recall, has been about studying the lesson; something most Bible teachers, more or less, do to some extent. I talked about the virtues of starting early on your lesson preparation and offered some suggestions for accomplishing this.

Then we looked at some "tools of the trade"—important resources to have available at your study desk. These included various versions of the Bible, concordances, Bible dictionaries, Bible atlases, and commentaries. We also considered the virtues of curriculum materials.

I hope I didn't sound too negative when I offered a warning against developing a fixation on some single source of help, such as a teacher's quarterly or lesson commentary. You have far too much creative potential to shackle yourself like that.

Before you zoom in on a single lesson, always survey the broader context in which the lesson appears. (Remember the chain-link fence?) This involves two things: First, become familiar with the book of the Bible in which you will be studying—its date, author, audience, purpose, and special characteristics. Second, preview the unit of lessons with which you will be working for several sessions. If your study material isn't already divided into units, create some units of your own.

I suggested keeping a notebook on upcoming lessons. I want to underscore that suggestion. Devote a page or two of notes to each lesson. (An outline for lesson previews was presented in one of the teaching lab activities.)

When you actually sit down to study a specific lesson, assuming that the background work has already been done, here is a suggested step-by-step procedure:

1. Read the Bible passage devotionally.
2. Read the Bible passage analytically.

(1) Use your pencil to mark unfamiliar words, key phrases, important ideas, and items which raise questions.

(2) Look up parallel passages with the help of center-column or marginal references.

(3) Ask yourself questions about the passage: What was said to whom? Why? With what result? What does it mean?

3. Use Bible-study tools.

(1) Use Bible dictionary and concordance to trace meanings of key words.

(2) Look up names of persons and places in a Bible dictionary.

(3) Use an atlas to locate places mentioned in the text.

(4) Consult commentaries for interpretation of the passage.

4. Consult curriculum materials.

5. Pull it together into a coherent design, identifying major ideas.

Finally, we thought about the role of the Spirit in the teacher's lesson preparation. The Spirit is more than a doctrine; he is our Guide into "all truth," transforming the printed text into a living message.

Many of the resources referred to in this chapter will be described in detail in the Appendix. There you will find specific guidance in the selection of concordances, Bible dictionaries, atlases, commentaries, and other Bible-study resources.

5
Teaching with Purpose

Once there was a father who loved his children very much. So, in order to safeguard their health, he stocked a cabinet with all kinds of medicines. Each morning, before the children went off to school, he would select a bottle of medicine from his cabinet and give each of them a dose. Each evening, just before bedtime, he would repeat the procedure. When a friend of the family asked the father about this rather unusual practice one evening, the father replied: "Well, medicine is supposed to be good for you, and I have remedies for many kinds of ailments in my medicine cabinet. The way I figure it, if I keep giving the children medicine regularly, it's bound to do them some good."

Don't worry about the children. The story is pure fiction. But it does illustrate a common attitude toward Bible teaching. "Just dispense portions of the Good Book, a dose here and a dose there, and it's bound to do some good, more or less, sooner or later."

When told by a church visitor, "We're trying to enroll new people in our Bible-study program," a young adult asked, "Why do you want to teach me the Bible? What will it do for me?" How would you have answered a question like that?

Faced with such questions, we find it hard not to respond in generalities. We might say, for example, "It will help you to live a better life." Better? In what respect? (Remember that some people think of a "better life" as one with more luxuries.) Or we might respond, "Bible study will help you cope with life's problems." And we believe this to be true, in a general sort of way; but what does it mean when you get down to specifics? Are we prepared to say that Bible study will actually help the clerk in a discount store cope with the grinding monotony of her job? Will it actually help the couple whose two-year-old marriage has turned into a living hell, or the aging man whose wife has been crippled by arthritis, or the high school graduate who doesn't know what to do with his life?

I happen to think that the answer to all these questions is yes. But only if we aim Bible study directly at such human problems. The "medicine cabinet" approach simply isn't purposeful enough. We can't claim that Bible study is good for everything in general unless we can demonstrate that it is good for some things in particular.

What I am saying here is caught up succinctly in the title of Findley Edge's helpful book for teachers, *Teaching for Results.* We ought to enter every Bible teaching situation looking for something definite to happen as a result of the lesson. How often has a frustrated schoolteacher, or parent, or office supervisor cried out, "We're going to have to change some things around here!" In a quite different sense, that should be the attitude of the Bible teacher. "We're here to make some changes!"

Most of the Bible was written to achieve specific results. Paul didn't write the letter to Philemon just to help his friend "live a better life" in general; he specifically wanted him to receive a runaway slave in a spirit of love. He didn't write what we know as the fifth chapter of 1 Corinthians to help that congregation "cope with life's problems." He insisted that they deal with a particular problem, the problem of high-handed immorality in their midst. The author of Hebrews wanted results; he wanted these Christians to recognize the sufficiency of Christ, so they would quit regressing into the Judaism from which they came. The writer of the Fourth Gospel left no doubt about the result which he hoped to produce. "But these are written that you may believe that Jesus is the Christ, the Son of God," he says, "and that believing you may have life in his name" (John 20:31, RSV). Hosea's purpose was equally specific. He wanted the people of his day to turn away from Baal worship and, with repentent hearts, serve Yahweh as the only true God.

Recall the significant events touched off by the rediscovery of the book of law in the Temple during the reign of King Josiah (2 Kings 22:3—23:25). The king was so moved by this discovery that he brought together "all the men of Judah and all the inhabitants of Jerusalem, and the priests and the prophets, all the people, both small and great; and he read in their hearing all the words of the book of the covenant which had been found in the house of the Lord" (23:2, RSV). They didn't go away that day congratulating themselves on having had a "nice lesson." No, that encounter with the Scriptures galvanized the hearers into action. The king and his people renewed their vows to the living God. Idolatrous priests were deposed, places of idolatrous worship destroyed, and worship of the true God was restored throughout the land.

Obviously, we can't expect such dramatic results from every Bible study session, but does this mean that we should expect nothing? Is there any reason why Bible study should not assuage grief, allay anxiety, restore hope, dispel fear, destroy idols, and propel God's people into acts of service? No, there's no reason why these things should not happen. But this immediately raises another question: Are we committed to teaching in such a way that they will happen?

What Kinds of Purpose?

Ask yourself, as you plan each lesson, "In what ways should people be changed as they study this portion of Scripture?" If teaching is "helping others to learn," as we said in the first chapter, every teacher is an agent of change. For change is the essense of learning. Without change there is no learning.

Sometimes the changes in people are dramatic. In a conference in New Mexico I met a beautiful young woman who had almost died in a suicide attempt two years earlier. Soon after her eighteenth birthday she had married into what she described as the "country club crowd" in her hometown, and life became a merry-go-round of cocktail parties, dances, and out-of-town conventions.

"Before I was twenty," she said, "I had tried everything in the book at least once." Then she talked about how life had become lonely and empty, and how she had tried to remedy this by drinking heavily and, later, using hard drugs. Finally, in despair, she had attempted to kill herself. "And I even failed at that," she said, with irony in her voice. "I was a complete failure at everything."

Then a friend invited her to attend a Bible class. Having nothing better to do, she went. It proved to be a turning point. Attracted by the warmth of fellowship and devotion in this circle of Christian learning, she returned the next Sunday, and for several weeks after that. Gradually, the Word of God kindled a flame within her, and she eventually received Jesus Christ as Savior and Lord.

As I stood in the doorway of our conference room, listening to this radiant young Christian tell her story, I could hardly believe that she had so recently been the human derelict she was describing.

The outcomes of Bible study will not always be so dramatic. Change in learners may take the form of subtle shifts in attitude, the deepening of conviction, a reorientation of values, or reformulations of doctrinal beliefs. The changes are often cognitive (mental) in nature, as is the case when learners study the historical setting of Nehemiah or when they memorize the books of the Bible in proper sequence.

Levels of learning. Studying a Bible passage may produce learning at more than one level. Consider the teaching of Jesus in John 14:1-4. This passage begins with the familiar words of assurance: "Let not your hearts be troubled; believe in God, believe also in me" (14:1, RSV). If class members learn the content of this passage, what, exactly, will they learn?

Suppose they memorize the passage, and can recite it word for word. Have they learned the content of the passage? Certainly, if that is the level of learning which you have in mind. Even though rote learning (memorization) seems to have gone out of style in this day and age, it still has a legitimate place in Bible study. People who can say with the psalmist, "I have laid up thy word in my heart" (119:11, RSV), will never be without a rich treasury of devotional resources. But it would be unfortunate if learning in Bible study were limited to the memorization of Scripture; for memorization does not always guarantee understanding.

Or suppose class members could explain in their own words what Jesus was saying to his disciples in this passage. Learning at the level of understanding is certainly an essential goal in Bible study activities. How poor we would be if we knew only the words of John 3:16 without understanding their relationship to the cross. What limited knowledge we would have if we could not explain the messianic implications of Isaiah 9:1-7 or the relationship between Psalm 51 and the moral lapse of King David. It was a question of no little significance when Philip asked the Ethiopian who was studying the prophecy of Isaiah, "Do you understand what you are reading?" (Acts 8:30, RSV).

Yet another level of learning would involve a knowledge of the background of this passage, its historical setting, and doctrinal significance. For instance, this particular conversation between Jesus and his disciples came at a very crucial time, in the very shadow of the cross. It apparently took place in the upper room where Jesus had assembled with his followers for a last meal. Little wonder he felt it especially urgent to say, "Let not your hearts be troubled." Soon they would be sheep without a shepherd; disheartened, confused, disillusioned. This knowledge helps us to understand not only the meaning of what he said, but also the emotional climate in which it was said and heard.

You could have yet another purpose in teaching this lesson. Consider, for a moment, not what Jesus said, but why he said it. When he said to his disciples, "Let not your hearts be troubled," what result was he looking for? Obviously, he wanted them to have untroubled hearts, hearts free of stress and anxiety. If Jesus wanted this for his disciples then, in the first century, doesn't he also want today's followers to have untroubled hearts? Wouldn't this be a fitting purpose for a lesson based on this portion of Scripture—to learn to face troubled times with confidence and faith in God?

Please note that we are now talking about learning in the realm of emotions. We can define faith in terms of words, concepts, ideas; but we *experience* faith in terms of emotional responses. The ability to have confidence in God in times of trouble depends to a great extent on how we feel about God and our relationship to him.

So, with respect to this one short passage (John 14:1-4),

we have identified four levels of learning, any of which could constitute a legitimate goal for teaching this lesson. First, memorizing the words. Second, explaining the meaning. Third, understanding the background. Fourth, cultivating an attitude of confidence in God even in the face of trying circumstances.

Purposes for Bible teaching. Actually, Bible teaching can be guided by a broad range of purposes which go beyond even the four levels of learning mentioned above. Look at some of the possibilities:

1. *Acquiring simple factual knowledge of the Bible.* Where are the Beatitudes found? Recite the Ten Commandments. Who was the father of King Solomon? Name the Synoptic Gospels. Who was the first Christian martyr? A large share of Bible-teaching activity is devoted to factual learning of this kind. It calls merely for the recollection of information without necessarily thinking about it in depth. A person may recite the Ten Commandments without understanding them, or identify the first Christian martyr without knowing the circumstances which contributed to his death.

We need to make a distinction between "simple" and "easy," however. The question, "Who was the first son of Isaiah?" calls for "simple factual information," but it isn't easy to accumulate a repertory of biblical information of this kind. One can hardly claim to be well-informed about the Bible without having a reasonable amount of such information. Yet, we would not want to limit our teaching goals to learning at this level, for this would produce walking encyclopedias of biblical information who have little insight into its meaning.

2. *Acquiring systematic factual knowledge of the Bible.* Another kind of factual Bible knowledge might be called

"systematic." The "simple" factual knowledge which we have been discussing consists of separate bits of information. "Systematic" factual knowledge consists of information which has a relationship to other information.

Biblical history provides prime examples of systematic knowledge. Knowing that Elijah was an Old Testament prophet is one thing; but knowing just where he fitted into the history of the divided kingdoms of Israel is quite another. The first bit of information could be called "simple factual knowledge"; but the second type of information is "systematic factual knowledge," because it has to do with the relationship of Elijah's ministry to a time sequence and to other historical figures.

Unfortunately, systematic Bible knowledge is all too rare, even among those who attend church regularly. So many people approach the Bible as they would a box of chocolates, picking out a goodie here and a goodie there, paying little attention to the overall design. The saying, "they sow the wind, and they shall reap the whirlwind," is a well-known adage, like Benjamin Franklin's proverbs. But to whom was this first said? By whom? And what was going on in the history of Israel at the time? These questions call for systematic biblical knowledge.

Here are some other examples: Which are the books of history in the Old Testament? Give two examples of Old Testament wisdom literature. In what chronological order were the epistles of Paul written? How do the four Gospels compare with one another? In what ways are they similar and in what ways do they differ? Why did Israel split into two kindgoms after the death of Solomon? Ask these questions of the typical Bible class member and you will need no further proof that systematic information about the Bible should receive greater emphasis in teaching goals.

3. *Understanding doctrinal themes.* A striking characteristic of the Bible is its marvelous unity. Written by numerous authors out of a diversity of cultural and linguistic backgrounds over a period of several centuries, the Scriptures comprise one grand story about God's activity in human history. Like golden threads, certain doctrinal themes run through the Bible from beginning to end. The doctrine of God as Creator, with which the biblical story opens, is echoed again and again. (See Ps. 102:25; Isa. 40:21 ff.; John 1:1; Acts 17:24.) And what we are told in John 3:16, "God so loved the world," is reflected in his reclamation of a sinful Adam (Gen. 3:9) as well as in the invitation with which Revelation closes, "And let him who is thirsty come, let him who desires take the water of life without price" (Rev. 22:17, RSV). Exploring such themes can be a richly rewarding form of Bible study.

To illustrate this further, let me ask you to work through the Scripture passages in the following exercise and to identify the doctrinal theme to which each set of references is related.

TEACHING LAB ACTIVITY NO. 16

Instructions: The three sets of Scripture references below are related to three doctrinal themes in the Bible. Read the references in each set, then, in a word or two, identify the doctrine which they seem to teach.

A. John 1:9-14; Rom. 1:3-4; Gal. 4:4; Phil. 2:7-8; Col. 1:22; 1 Tim. 3:16; Heb. 2:14; 1 John 1:1-3. These Scriptures are related to the doctrine of _____.

B. Rom. 1:18; Gen. 1:23-24; 6:5-7; Ezra 8:22; Pss. 2:11; 21:9; Rom. 2:5; Eph. 5:6; Rev. 14:10; 15:1. These

Scriptures are related to the doctrine of _____
_____.

   C. Prov. 2:1-5; Hos. 4:1,6; 6:6; John 17:3; Rom. 3:10-
11; 11:33; 1 Cor. 15:34; Col. 1:9-10; 2 Pet. 1:2-3. These
Scriptures are related to the doctrine of _____
_____.

Teaching goals in this area of learning have to do with
more than factual knowledge. They call for an understanding
of some of the great theological concepts imbedded in the
pages of Scripture. This kind of understanding is so important to the development of mature Christian disciples.

4. *Mastering techniques of Bible study.* Your purposes in
teaching will include training in methods of Bible study as
well as instruction in the content of Scripture. A Bible
teacher should try to help each learner become a competent
student of the Scriptures. If there were no other reason,
that would be reason enough to have learners use their Bibles, concordances, marginal references, and maps of Bible
lands in class.

This purpose combines nicely with other teaching aims.
Suppose you were to lead a group study of one of the doctrinal themes mentioned earlier. You might read a series of
Scriptures from prepared teaching notes. But if class members look up the Scripture passages themselves, they not
only will benefit from the content but also will become more
familiar with the use of their Bibles in the process.

5. *Learning principles of interpretation.* Competence in
Bible study also requires a knowledge of certain principles
of interpretation.

We've already mentioned the importance of anchoring
interpretations of Scripture in the historical context. Let's

think about a rule for interpreting New Testament parables. The rule is this: Each parable was designed to teach a single truth; and one's interpretation of the parable should focus on this central truth. Jesus always used a parable to get across a certain point in his teaching, and the modern interpreter has no right to make the parable mean a dozen other things. In the story which we call the parable of the prodigal son (Luke 15:11-32), Jesus was answering the criticism which is reported in verse 2: "This man receives sinners and eats with them" (RSV). The point of this parable is that the Pharisees and scribes were behaving exactly like the elder brother in the story. Rather than being glad that sinners were "coming home" to the father, they were standing back and pouting about it.

You could do other things with this parable, of course. You could make a great deal of the fact that the younger son "went into a far country" and "wasted his substance in riotous living." That would be a dandy way to lambast sin of all kinds. The problem is, that isn't what Jesus meant by the parable. Ironically, the parable actually indicts "moral" people who sit on cushioned church pews and snub sinners much more than it does those people on the other side of the stained-glass windows.

6. *Drawing rules of conduct from Scripture.* In the first century A.D., as Christianity spread across North Africa, Asia, and other parts of the Mediterranean world, one of the most important purposes of teaching in the churches was to instruct new converts in the Christian way of life. Many converts had come straight out of pagan cultures, and it was difficult for them to adjust to the new kind of life-style required by the gospel of Jesus Christ.

Numerous passages of Scripture reflect this concern. "Put to death therefore what is earthly in you: immorality, impur-

ity, passion, evil desire, and covetousness," wrote Paul to
the Christians at Colossae, "in these you once walked, when
you lived in them. But now put them all away: anger, wrath,
malice, slander, and foul talk from your mouth. Do not lie
to one another, seeing that you have put off the old nature
with its practices and have put on the new nature" (Col.
3:5-10, RSV). (See also Gal. 5:16-24; Eph. 4:17-32; 5:1-5.)

Jesus himself was greatly concerned about conduct, as
even a casual reading of the Sermon on the Mount (Matt.
5—7) will show. He spoke in terms of profound principles,
rather than cataloging endless rules of behavior as the Pharisees and scribes did. This was the hallmark of his ethical
teaching. It is so much easier to follow a rule, such as, "Don't
falsify your income tax return," than it is to translate principles, such as, "Seek ye first the kingdom of God and his
righteousness," into patterns of everyday conduct. That's
why a Bible study class should provide a forum for exploring
the meaning of such teachings.

The need for "instruction in righteousness" is as great
today as it was in the first century, and this purpose will
often be at the top of your list of goals for Bible studies.
However, it is a purpose not easily achieved. People would
much rather listen to nice "safe" comments on the Scriptures
than change their conduct. This kind of teaching calls for
something more than explanations of the text. Learners must
grapple with ethical truth through dialogue, experimentation, and testing in the crucible of human experience in
order to translate it into the language of daily relationships.

One Sunday I was walking out of a men's Bible class with
a friend, a good lawyer and part-time politician. He said,
"You know, I had heard those words of Jesus, 'love your
enemies,' all my life; but I never realized how hard it would
be to put that into practice until about a year ago, when I

decided to really give it a try." He told me about attempting to change his relationship with a "political enemy," a man who had been a longtime opponent in county politics. "No matter what he did, I determined to respond in a loving way," my friend said. "At first it was very difficult, because he continued to tell lies about me and do everything he could to damage me. But, after several months, things began to change; and now, as incredible as it seems, we are even beginning to develop a friendship."

There was only one thing wrong with that conversation. It should have taken place in the Bible class. Christians need to do a lot of talking with one another about things like that as they learn from the Scriptures how to live as kingdom people.

7. *Developing biblical attitudes.* I forget now what the issue was. A seminary classmate and I were arguing about some doctrinal matter (a favorite indoor sport of seminarians). At one point in the conversation, he drew himself to his full height, gave me his most disdainful look, and said, "Well, of course, I always make it a point to adopt the biblical attitude in all situations." I knew he was jesting, of course, mimicking the modern-day Pharisees who justify anything they want to do by calling it biblical. But it isn't just a joking matter. The Bible does speak of attitudes which God's people are obligated to incorporate into their personalities.

When the psalmist says, "How sweet are thy words to my taste, sweeter than honey to my mouth!" (119:103, RSV), he is expressing, not a doctrinal belief, but an attitude. When Paul writes to his friends in Christ at Philippi, "For God is my witness, how I yearn for you all with the affection of Christ Jesus" (Phil. 1:8), he is revealing an attitude. When Jesus blesses "those who hunger and thirst for righteousness" (Matt. 5:6, RSV), he is talking about what is basically an attitude toward God. The steady faith of Abraham, the moral stamina of Joseph, the invincible courage of Daniel, and the outgoing love of the woman who washed the feet of Jesus with her tears; these all are attitudes.

"Casting all your care upon him," "fear not little flock," "be ye kind one to another, tender-hearted, forgiving one another," "blessed are the merciful," and "trust in the Lord" are only a few of the many Scriptures which urge us to adopt certain attitudes.

What this all adds up to is that the cultivation of Christian attitudes must be one of the major goals of Bible study, if we are to be true to the deep concerns expressed in the Scriptures themselves. And, frankly, this is one of the hardest things you'll ever attempt to do as a teacher. For attitudes are bound up with the emotions and emotions aren't easily altered. It's one thing to discuss the parable of the good Samaritan in class; but it's another thing to lead a class member to have a more positive attitude toward the guy next door whose Great Danes bark and howl all night. It's easy to marvel at the faith of Abraham; but it's a little harder to maintain an attitude of faith when someone you love goes into the hospital for exploratory surgery.

TEACHING LAB ACTIVITY NO. 17

Instructions: Now that we've examined seven distinct purposes which might be included in your Bible teaching goals, it's time to practice recognizing them.

First, I'll list the seven purposes mentioned above:

1. Acquiring simple factual knowledge of the Bible
2. Acquiring systematic factual knowledge of the Bible
3. Understanding doctrinal themes

4. Mastering techniques of Bible study
5. Applying principles of interpretation
6. Drawing rules of conduct from Scripture
7. Developing biblical attitudes

Next, I'll give you several sample teaching goals. Your job is to decide which of the purposes listed above fits each sample teaching goal. In each case, just write the number of the purpose in front of the sample goal.

Here are two sample items:

__6__ Y. After reading a case study which describes an on-the-job conflict and presents three possible courses of action, class members should be able to identify the course of action which most reflects the teaching of Jesus in Matthew 5:38-48.

__4__ Z. By the end of this session, every class member should be able to use a concordance to look up an incomplete Scripture quotation.

Ready to go? All right. Here are the sample teaching goals:

_____ A. Each learner should be able to name five New Testament books written by Paul.

_____ B. As a result of this lesson, the members of our class who are not Christians should show a willingness to discuss the meaning of a commitment to Christ with me when I approach them individually afterwards.

_____ C. By the end of this session, each member will be able to locate in his own Bible at least three Scriptures which are related to the exaltation of Christ.

_____ D. Given brief descriptions of five events in the life of Israel, class members should be able to arrange them in proper chronological order, then rank them in the order of their importance.

_____ E. Each class member should be able to report

on the central meaning of a parable of Jesus which
has been assigned a week in advance.

_____ F. After this session, a class member should be
able to explain how to use a center-column reference.

_____ G. Learners should be able to give the names
of the original twelve apostles.

_____ H. Before the next class session, each member
should be able to draw up his or her own "Ten Rules
for Family Living" based on Paul's description of *agapé*
in 1 Corinthians 13:4-7.

_____ I. As a result of this lesson on worship, class
members should show more positive feelings about
worship by voluntarily improving their attendance
record at Sunday worship services.

_____ J. Each class member should be able to suggest
seven Scriptures suitable for a Christmas service.

_____ K. At the conclusion of this unit on Paul's missionary journeys, learners should be able to state at
least three characteristics of his overall missionary strategy.

Now, let's compare our answers . . . .

We're not concerned here with how many items you
got "right" or "wrong." What we are concerned with
is understanding the different kinds of purposes which
might become Bible teaching goals. Some items could
have more than one answer, depending on your point
of view. With this understanding, let me tell you which
answers I chose, and why.

A. Simple factual Bible knowledge. Agreed?

B. "Willingness" is an attitude. So is an interest in
becoming a Christian. I would say that this is an example of "developing biblical attitudes."

C. The three Scriptures are related to the same
theme, the exaltation of Christ. That's number 3 in
our list.

D. You might say that this sample goal calls for simple factual knowledge. You might. But this is an example of *systematic* factual knowledge. Why? Because the learner couldn't possibly deal with the five historical events separately. They have to be related to one another, in two different ways. They must be treated "systematically."

E. Did you say "applying principles of interpretation"? Right! It's the same principle we looked at earlier. Every parable has one central meaning.

F. Number 4, obviously.

G. Simple factual knowledge, again. But aren't the facts related? Well, yes, in the sense that they are members of the same group; but, no, not in the sense that historical events are interrelated. The key is that the twelve names can be given separately, in whatever order you wish; you can even leave out one or two without affecting the others. You can't do that with systematic knowledge.

H. The words, "draw up," might have tipped you off. This is an example of "drawing rules of conduct from Scripture."

I. You could easily substitute the word *attitudes* for the word *feelings* in this sample goal. The improved church attendance reflects an improvement of attitudes toward worship. So, this one is number 7.

J. Number 3, "understanding doctrinal themes." My assumption is that the Scriptures used in this service would be related to a Christmas theme, such as "Incarnation" or "The Messiah." The learners would have to understand this doctrinal theme in order to choose Scriptures intelligently.

K. This one was a little difficult, I'll admit. But you can eliminate 1, 4, 5, 6, and 7 fairly easily. And the information called for isn't really doctrinal. It is factual knowledge of Paul's missionary strategy, but it is systematic factual knowledge, because the learner must

pull together what she or he knows about these journeys, then discover some overall patterns.

Some Characteristics of Teaching Goals

Look again at those sample teaching goals in the teaching
lab activity above. They are phrased in various ways, but
they have some characteristics in common.

Goals are stated as learning outcomes. There's an old story
about a good citizen out for his morning walk who came
upon some stonemasons plying their trade. "What are you
doing, my good man?" he asked one. The workman looked
up and replied, in an indifferent sort of way, "I'm layin'
stones." Walking a bit further, the man came upon another
stonemason and asked the same question, "What are you
doing?" But this second workman replied, "Sir, I'm building
a cathedral!"

The story is a popular pulpit illustration but I want to
use it to point out something about teaching goals. They
should be stated in terms of the end product (the cathedral)
rather than the teacher's activity (laying stones). And what
is the end product of teaching? Why, learning, of course.
Your teaching goals should describe a learning outcome,
rather than how you plan to make learning happen.

• *Teaching activity:* Present a lecture on the characteristics of apocalyptic literature in the Bible. *Learning outcome:*
Be able to describe the characteristics of apocalyptic literature.

• *Teaching activity:* Teach learners how to use a concordance. *Learning outcome:* Be able to use a concordance to
look up incomplete biblical quotations.

• *Teaching activity:* Lead the class in the study of Scriptures related to the second coming of Christ. *Learning outcome:* Be able to locate at least three Scriptures related to the second coming of Christ.

• *Teaching activity:* Show a filmstrip on the life of King David. *Learning outcome:* Be able to outline the major events in the life of King David.

When you think of your teaching goals for a particular session, or for a unit of study, think in terms of what class members ought to learn.

Goals are stated in specific terms. Look over the key verbs used to describe learning outcomes in the sample goals listed in Teaching Lab Activity No. 17. "Identify," "use," "name," "locate," "arrange," "draw-up," "state"—all are concrete action verbs. Compare those with verbs such as "understand," "know," and "develop a knowledge of." The first group of verbs describe actions which you can see. But you can't see "understanding," can you? "Sure, I can," you might say, "I can tell that someone understands by the way she nods her head and says, 'uh-huh,' when I'm trying to explain something. But, if you say that, you've just proved my point. You don't actually see the "understanding." You see the head-nodding and hear the "uh-huh." And that makes you *assume* that understanding is there. A secretary can nod her head and say "uh-huh" all she wants to, but if the boss wants her to communicate an extremely urgent message to someone, he will say, "Now, read it back to me, so I'll be sure you have it right." Reading the message back is a concrete way to demonstrate understanding of it.

The key question is this: "If my class members really do learn what I want them to learn, how will I know it?" If they "develop an understanding" or "deepen appreciation" of something, you might not be aware of it. But if they "locate on a map," or "write definitions," or "arrange in proper sequence," you can tell when they are doing that.

In the following teaching lab activity you'll find some sample teaching goals which contain concrete action verbs, describing learning outcomes which you can actually see or hear. On the other hand, there are some sample goals which contain less specific verbs, describing outcomes which you can only assume have taken place. See if you can tell the difference between these two kinds of goals.

TEACHING LAB ACTIVITY NO. 18

Instructions: Place a check mark (✔) in front of each sample teaching goal which contains a concrete action verb. Remember, a "concrete action verb" describes a learning result which you can actually see or hear.

_____ A. Learners should be able to draw a diagram showing the layout of the Temple of Jerusalem during the time of Jesus.

_____ B. Learners should have a deeper appreciation of Hebrew poetry as a result of this study of the Psalms.

_____ C. Upon completing this unit of study, learners should have a broader understanding of Old Testament prophecy.

_____ D. Upon completing this unit of study, learners should be able to describe five major characteristics of Old Testament prophecy.

_____ E. This lesson will help class members understand the origin of the Bible's wisdom literature.

_____ F. Given a list of Scripture references, learners should be able to identify the references related to the doctrine of atonement.

(Note: I would vote for goals A, D, and F. Which did you choose?)

Goals should reflect different levels and kinds of learning. Let me tell you a story about three Bible classes. In the first class, the teacher started the lesson by saying, "All right, now, I'd like for each of you to read one of the verses in the lesson passage and share with us whatever ideas it brings to mind." In the second, the teacher went through the story of the raising of Lazarus, with special emphasis on Jesus' command, "Unbind him, and let him go" (John 11:44, RSV). Then he said, "Let's talk about the things that are binding us in our lives. In what ways do we need to be unbound?" In the third class, the teacher began by saying, "As you know, today's lesson, based on Ephesians 5:21—6:4, is about family life. So I have invited Dr. _____ to visit our class to talk with us about family relations."

These classes, quite different from one another in some ways, had one thing in common. They all ignored the meaning of Scripture in its historical context. To share "whatever ideas" a verse of Scripture "brings to mind" is not the same thing as trying to understand the message of the Bible. And "talking about the things that are binding us in our lives" doesn't quite get at the meaning of the biblical text. One of the surest ways for us to lose the Word of God even as we hold the Bible in our hands is to use it as a conversation piece, rather than a document worthy of serious study.

On the other hand, a purely academic knowledge of the Bible—its history, language, and literary forms—can leave a person untouched by its deeper truth, the truth which gets into the fiber of one's being.

The Scriptures can be known at several levels of understanding. Committing the words of Scripture to memory can provide food for devotional thought and expand the vocabulary of prayer. The moral precepts of the Bible can shed light on one's path in a world which is often uncertain about right and wrong. Its great doctrinal themes can expand one's awareness of God and his will for his people. When we open ourselves to the Word at the deeper levels of our beings, it can become a source of life-changing truth, "discerning the thoughts and intentions of the heart."

And so should it be with our teaching goals. In a Bible class, learning should take place at all of these levels, not all at once. No single lesson lends itself to all of these purposes. Sometimes you will want to focus on basic factual information, sometimes on details of interpretation. And, sometimes, you will want to help your class members master broad concepts in biblical thought, or to explore the meaning of scriptural teaching where it touches real life. The important thing is to avoid getting into a rut where purposes in teaching are always the same.

Keep in mind what was said in chapter 2 about classifying learning as "cognitive" or "affective." Remember that *cognitive learning* has to do with mental activity—thinking, memorizing, gaining knowledge, acquiring concepts, and *affective learning* has to do with emotions, attitudes, and feelings.

No learning is purely cognitive or affective, of course. Cognitive learning generally has some bearing on emotions and attitudes, and affective learning certainly has some relationship to knowledge and ideas. But most of your goals in Bible teaching will be *primarily* cognitive, or *primarily* affective.

The key to classifying them is to ask the question, "Is the kind of learning suggested by this goal mostly cognitive, or mostly affective?"

The purpose of the following teaching lab activity is to help you sharpen your ability to classify learning outcomes as cognitive or affective.

TEACHING LAB ACTIVITY NO. 19

Instructions: Read each statement below and decide whether it has to do primarily with *cognitive* learning or primarily with *affective* learning. If cognitive, write "C" in front of the statement; if affective, write "A" in front of it.

_____ 1. Every member of the class learned to recite the books of the New testament in proper order.

_____ 2. After the unit on worship, there seemed to be an increased spirit of reverence during devotionals.

_____ 3. The teacher wanted class members to show a Christlike concern for people often ignored by society, such as the handicapped and the mentally retarded.

_____ 4. "I want you to learn to explain the meaning of each of the Beatitudes," the teacher said.

_____ 5. The class learned to trace the first missionary journey of Paul on a map of the Mediterranean world.

_____ 6. During the study of the Gospel of John, more and more of the men committed themselves to personal witnessing in daily life.

_____ 7. "At the end of this session, I want each of you to be able to write a statement explaining what a Christian's attitude should be toward abortion, war, and capital punishment, in light of the Sixth Commandment."

(Now let's compare answers: 1-C; 2-A; 3-A; 4-C; 5-C; 6-A; 7-C.)

Why bother to think about teaching goals in terms of cognitive and affective learning? In teaching, it helps to know whether you are trying to get results in the area of ideas and factual knowledge, or in the area of attitudes and emotions, because you must use different approaches to teaching for these two kinds of learning. In other words, if you know where you're going, you'll know better how to get there.

Writing Teaching Goals

Goal-setting is the starting place for lesson-planning. You can't very well plan a journey if you don't know where you want to end up. A golfer wouldn't think of hitting the ball without pinpointing the location of the next green. A carpenter doesn't start sawing and hammering unless he knows what the finished house is supposed to look like. And you can't "teach with purpose" unless you have a purpose. The first step in planning a lesson is to write your teaching goal (or goals). I want to suggest a process for doing this.

Start with the Bible passage. If we're going to teach the Bible, the Bible must shape our teaching goals. Serving up our latest thoughts on the state of the world, suitably decorated with a few verses of Scripture, isn't exactly the same as teaching the sacred Word. We must let the Word speak to us before we can have a sure word to speak to others.

But a Bible passage can speak to us in more ways than one. Look at Psalm 8. It contains two distinct themes, either of which could provide ample material for a one-hour Bible study session. The first is caught up in the opening words:

"O Lord, our Lord, how majestic is thy name in all the earth!" (v. 1, RSV). What a splendid foundation for a lesson on worship! The second theme is introduced by the question, "What is man that thou art mindful of him?" (v. 4). This paves the way for a fruitful study of the biblical doctrine of man.

Acts 15 is another good illustration. This is the chapter which tells us about the crucial conference in Jerusalem where Christians who believed in salvation through faith in Christ alone ran head-on into the Judaizers who wanted to add Jewish rituals to the requirements for salvation. I remember preparing to lead a study of this chapter once. As I explored the biblical material, at least four possible teaching goals surfaced.

First, my class could easily use all the available time just analyzing the controversy which gave rise to the Jerusalem conference. And this would be time well spent, because the question concerning the relationship of Judaism to Christianity was one of the pivotal issues in the book of Acts.

On the other hand, what an excellent opportunity this would be to focus on the Christian doctrine of salvation. The first-century Judaizers weren't the only ones who have tried to add to the simple requirement of faith in Christ. There are those who say, "Believe in Christ and get yourself baptized by an approved brand-name minister if you want to be saved." That's not too different from the stance of the Judaizers who said, "Believe in Christ and be circumcised and thou shalt be saved."

But I realized, as I prepared to teach this lesson, that this chapter contained another powerful truth. The Judaizers were actually saying to the Gentile Christians, "You aren't welcome in our church unless you become Jews like us." We encounter this kind of exclusivism in other forms today.

"You aren't welcome in our church unless your skin is the right color and you come from the right ethnic background." Sometimes the requirement has to do with wearing nice clothes.

Finally, Acts 15 presents an interesting study in church polity. How does a church go about resolving a controversial issue? What are the appropriate roles of "clergy" and "laity"? Who makes a final decision? How is the decision made? This passage suggests some very definite answers to questions like these.

You can understand my difficulty. Here I was, faced with the task of teaching a Bible lesson which could go in four different directions. What do you do in a case like that? Some teachers would simply try to cover all four emphases. But that's a mistake, unless you have a lot more time than most Bible classes have in a weekly study session. (It's not uncommon for classes in church teaching programs to have forty-five minutes or less for actual Bible study, after greetings, record-taking, announcements, and empty chatter.) If you undertake too much in too little time, you'll end up covering a lot of material superficially, but nothing in depth.

The only alternative is to be selective; to do just what you would do in a cafeteria with several tempting dishes spread out before you. Just choose the one which is more tempting than the rest. How do you make such a choice? This is where you must bring in another element—the needs and interests of class members.

Consider needs and interests of class members. Remember the discussion in chapter 3, where we considered the importance of knowing the persons who sit under your teaching? That kind of knowledge really pays off when you are in the process of formulating teaching goals. You find your teaching goals where the biblical message touches the life and experience of the learner.

We might illustrate that like this:

See 3:11, 18;
4: 1-3
Deut. 1:34-35

written to
Christians?

The Bible?
or
the "Word"
in John 1?

?
.

The Word:

Cleanses-
Eph. 5:26
Saves - 1 Pet. 1:23
Works in believers - 1 Thess. 2:13

11 Let us therefore strive to enter that rest, that no one fall by the same sort of disobedience. 12 For the word of God is living and active, sharper than any two-edged sword, piercing to the division of soul and spirit, of joints and marrow, and discerning the thoughts and intentions of the heart. 13 And before him no creature is hidden, but all are open and laid bare to the eyes of him with whom we have to do.

?

acts 7: 38
Isa. 49:2
Rev. 1:16
(Look
this up.)
Ps. 33:13-15
Rom. 14:12

The Bible covers a wide range of material, all of it important in the sense that it constitutes a part of God's revelation to humanity. But, at any given time, certain portions of the biblical text may seem more relevant to the learner's experience than other portions. A person who is suffering from the pangs of a new grief may respond more to Jesus' words, "Blessed are those who mourn, for they shall be comforted" (Matt. 5:4 RSV) than to the long genealogy in the first chapter of Matthew.

One bright Sunday in June, a few years ago, I attended a men's Bible class in a California church. The lesson that day had something to do with the reign of King David. I don't remember it too well. But I do remember how one member of that class, a man whom I knew personally, was hurting inside. Not long before, he had been drawn into a fight with a twenty-year-old son who had become very abusive, and he had finally thrown his son out of the house. It had been a bad scene, a heartbreaking experience. I sat in the class thinking about how deeply my friend could have identified with the heartcry of the grief-stricken king of Israel, "O my son Absalom, my son, my son Absalom!" But the teacher, oblivious to the problem, went on rambling through a monotonous recital of historical data connected with David's reign.

There are large areas of the "learner's life-experience" which do not overlap with a particular Bible lesson. Once I heard a Christian labor union leader complain, "On last Monday morning I had to decide whether or not to call a strike that would affect thousands of people; and on Sunday I sat through our Bible class hoping to find some guidance that would help me make that hard decision. But I found none." In a broad sense, that man's point was well-taken. The Bible ought to be a "lamp unto our feet" and a "light to our path" in the crucible of everyday living. But, on the other hand, learners can hardly expect to find an exact "fit" between their current needs and the biblical material in each lesson. The teacher's responsibility in selecting goals for a lesson is to identify the areas of overlap between the biblical message and the needs and interests of learners.

"Needs" an "interests" aren't always the same thing, by the way. Learners sometimes have needs which are not reflected in their current interests. A Christian might need to become more involved in meaningful worship experiences without being aware of that need. Class members might need to be confronted with the demands of discipleship without being particularly interested in the subject. In fact, their lack of interest might be precisely the thing which most points up the need.

Write a preliminary goal. You have thought about the

content of the Bible passage in relation to the needs and interests of your class members. Now it's time to write down what you would like to see happen as a result of this lesson; a preliminary goal. It is "preliminary" because you might want to revise it. Don't be too concerned, just yet, about using those "action-verbs" we talked about earlier. Just put down on paper what you would like to see class members learn in this session.

For instance, in connection with a study of Psalm 8, I might say of myself, "My class members really do need to hear the words of verse 6. God has given us dominion over all the works of his hands. Having dominion means not being dominated by things, such as alcohol, drugs, tobacco, or an over-abundance of food." Then I might write down this preliminary goal: "As a result of this lesson I want my class members to resolve to be in control of the material world, rather than let the material world control them."

Analyze the preliminary goal. After writing a preliminary goal for the lesson, think through the goal by answering each of these questions:

1. Does this goal grow out of the Bible passage?

2. Does this goal reflect needs and interests of class members?

3. Is this goal important?

4. Does this goal call for learning which is primarily cognitive (mental and intellectual) or affective (emotional and attitudinal)?

5. Is it reasonable to assume that this goal can be accomplished, given the time available for this lesson?

6. If the learning called for by this goal does take place, how will I know it?

For the sake of illustration, let me tell you how I would answer each of these questions in connection with the preliminary goal mentioned earlier in relation to a lesson on Psalm 8.

1. *Does this goal grow out of the Bible passage?* Yes, definitely. The psalmist's primary answer to the question, "What is man?" is that man has been given dominion over all created things.

2. *Does this goal reflect needs and interests of class members?* Yes. Like most middle-aged adults, my class members are continually faced with the temptation to let material things master them—food, drink, tobacco, drugs, and the like.

3. *Is this goal important?* Yes. Far from being incidental, these matters are central to the happiness, welfare, and Christian commitment of my class members.

4. *Does this goal call for learning which is primarily cognitive or affective?* Hmm. Let's see. The key verb in my preliminary goal is "to resolve." I want the men in my class to "resolve to be in control of the material world." That's really a matter of attitude. Some of the learning will be cognitive, of course. We will have to spend some time developing the psalmist's thought, especially what is meant by "having dominion" over things. And that's cognitive learning. But the real payoff I'm looking for is in the area of attitude, a personal commitment.

5. *Can this goal be accomplished?* No one can guarantee that it will happen, of course, but there should be enough time to develop the lesson and lead members to the point of making a commitment of this kind.

6. *If the learning called for in this goal does take place, how will I know it?* This is a hard one. I'll have to give it a lot more thought. But maybe I could ask class members to report in a month on what they did as a result of this lesson. I could give each person a self-addressed envelope

and a sheet of paper, ask them to write down what they intend to do as a result of the lesson now; then, in a month, add a report on how well they carried it out. That might work.

Rewrite the goal for greater clarity. Thus far, we haven't paid much attention to the wording of the goal. But now is the time to rewrite it for greater clarity. Try, especially, to use the kind of action verb discussed earlier.

Recall my preliminary goal: "As a result of this lesson I want my class members to resolve to be in control of the material world, rather than let the material world control them." A little vague, I would say. In the first place, "resolve" doesn't name any tangible action. How do you know when a person has "resolved"? Also, what does it mean to "control the material world"? That needs to be more specific.

Here's how the goal might be revised to improve its clarity: "During the course of this lesson, class members will specify ways to carry out the divine mandate to 'have dominion' over the material world, and each member will adopt one of these as a personal goal during the coming month."

TEACHING LAB ACTIVITY NO. 20

Instructions: As they say, practice makes perfect. While the process for writing teaching goals is fresh in mind, let's practice using it. Since it would take quite a bit of time to start a Bible lesson from scratch, I want to suggest a passage of Scripture and a preliminary teaching goal based on that passage. Your task will be to analyze the goal, applying the six questions already suggested.

The Bible passage: Galatians 5:16-24 (Please read this passage in your Bible before proceeding further.)

Preliminary goal: "As a result of this study, I want my class members to be able to name the 'works of the flesh' and the 'fruits of the Spirit.' "

Answer these questions:

1. Does the goal grow out of the Bible passage?
2. Does the goal reflect the needs and interests of the members of your own class?
3. Is the goal important?
4. Does the goal call for cognitive or affective learning?
5. Can the goal be accomplished?
6. If the learning called for in this goal takes place, how can the teacher know it?

After working through all the questions, compare your responses to the ones I have recorded in the following notes:

(1) Yes, the goal comes straight out of the passage. (2) You'll have to answer this, since I don't know the members of your class. (3) I'm dubious about this one. Any information about the Bible is important, I suppose. But I'm not sure that memorizing these "works of the flesh" and "fruits of the Spirit" is going to mean much. In my opinion, a more significant goal would be to help class members understand their meaning in terms of daily life. (4) Cognitive. No doubt about it. (5) Sure. No reason why the average class member couldn't learn to list these "works" and "fruits" in a single session. (6) This wouldn't be hard. They could be written down or recited. Maybe a "final exam" at the end of the session would be in order.

Teaching with Purpose—a Summary

This chapter began with an appeal for purposeful teaching; "teaching for results," as my friend Findley Edge has put it. The key thoughts in the chapter may be summarized as follows:

• We should be as specific as possible when thinking about those purposes which we hope to accomplish through Bible study.

• Any Bible passage may be taught and learned at several different levels. Thus, purposes for Bible teaching may include any of the following: (1) acquiring simple factual knowledge, (2) acquiring systematic factual knowledge, (3) understanding doctrinal themes, (4) mastering techniques of Bible study, (5) learning principles of interpretation, (6) drawing rules of conduct from Scripture, and (7) developing biblical attitudes.

• The Bible teacher's purposes are expressed through teaching goals. Goals should (1) be stated as learning outcomes, rather than teaching activities, (2) be stated in specific terms, and (3) reflect different levels and kinds of learning.

• To write a teaching goal for a given lesson, the teacher should (1) start with the Bible passage, (2) consider needs and interests of class members, (3) write a preliminary goal, (4) analyze the preliminary goal by asking pertinent questions about it, and (5) rewrite the goal for greater clarity.

Writing a teaching goal is the first step in developing a teaching plan. And that's what we will take up in the next chapter.

6
How to Develop a Plan for Teaching

In one seminary course, students are required to submit carefully developed lesson plans for Bible study sessions. Then they teach Bible classes in nearby churches, using those lesson plans. Not long ago, during an evaluation of this project, a student said, "I have never had to prepare a written lesson plan before; but I certainly will from now on. It gave me so much confidence, because I knew what I was doing. I never realized that teaching could be such a joy."

She had discovered a secret that I wish every Bible teacher could know; the joy of teaching with a well-prepared lesson plan. Sure, it takes time to plan a lesson well. But the pay-off makes it all worthwhile. A good lesson plan helps you to use time in the classroom wisely. It gives you a sense of direction and helps you keep the study session on target. Most importantly, careful planning frees a teacher from that feeling of uncertainty, that gnawing anxiety that something might go wrong. The teacher's lesson plan is like a coach's game plan, a general's battle strategy, an architect's blueprints. It's your best insurance against the unpredictable.

What a Lesson Plan Is—and Is Not

Some teachers go into class armed with an outline of the Bible passage which looks like this:
    I. A plot against Daniel (Dan. 6:1-9)
    II. Daniel's faithfulness to God (6:10)
    III. Daniel cast into the lions' den (6:11-18)

IV. God delivers Daniel (6:19-24)

V. God is glorified (6:25-28)

Or they might prepare a set of notes on "points to bring out in the lesson," like this:

6:3—Godliness and personal excellence go hand in hand.

6:4—Success in leadership often breeds jealousy.

6:10—A regular devotional life was at the heart of Daniel's religion.

6:12—The world has many ways of interfering with one's prayer life.

6:22—The safest place in the world is in the center of God's will.

6:25-27—The faithfulness of righteous people brings glory to God.

Outlines and notes like these may be helpful, but they are not lesson plans. They refer only to the content of the Bible passage, or thoughts related to the passage. A lesson plan is a design for teaching the content of the passage. A content outline tells what is to be taught; a lesson plan tells how it is to be taught. A lesson plan is a strategy for action, an outline of teaching-learning procedures which are to be used in a Bible-study session.

A lesson plan for leading a study of the sixth chapter of Daniel might look something like this:

I. Begin by asking this question: "Suppose you were living under a totalitarian government which made it strictly illegal to worship God publicly, and that violations of this law could result in imprisonment or even death. Would it be better to brazenly defy the law, and go on worshiping publicly, or to worship God secretly in your home and with friends while avoiding public worship?" Let class members respond.

II. Ask class members to scan Daniel 6:1-28 in study teams of two, with these two questions in mind: (1) How would

Daniel answer the question which we have just discussed?
(2) If he could have prayed secretly, why do you think he
went on praying where he could easily be overheard? After
about five minutes, give study teams a chance to report their
conclusions.

III. Organize class into discussion groups of four. Using
Daniel 6 as a background for the group discussion, ask each
group to use these questions as a guide: (1) What happened?
(2) Why did it happen? (3) What was the result? (4) What
does it mean in terms of principles which are applicable
to our lives? (Allow about twenty minutes for the group
discussion.)

IV. Let groups report their answers to the fourth question.
List these on the chalkboard.

V. Close the session by letting members discuss this question in their groups of four: At what times in my own life
do I come closest to experiencing the dilemma which Daniel
faced as a result of the king's decree? (In other words, when
is my own loyalty to God most put to the test?)

Compare this lesson plan to the content outline presented
earlier. Do you see how they differ? The content outline
reflects what is in the Bible passage. The lesson plan tells
how the lesson is to be taught.

The Essential Ingredients

In curriculum periodicals you will find a variety of lesson
plan outlines. A typical outline will look something like this:

    I. Stimulating interest
   II. Leading the Bible study
 III. Highlighting eternal truths
 IV. Applying the lesson to life
  V. Previewing the next lesson

Although I have no argument against such outlines, I am

wary of those who insist that every lesson should be crammed into the same mold. I have never seen a lesson plan outline which fits every lesson.

When you get down to the "bare-bones" essentials, your lesson plan must accomplish three things. First, you must make the learners want to study the lesson. Second, you must introduce study activities designed to help them get something out of the Bible passage. Third, you must clinch the lesson. Let's look at each of these functions more closely.

Grabbing the learner's attention. The first function of the lesson plan, making the learner want to study the lesson, has to do with kindling an interest in the lesson. As you know, class members don't always dash into the room with the day's lesson foremost in their minds. They are thinking about jobs, family problems, recreational interests, and social relations. Some are preoccupied with financial pressures, gloomy headlines, physical discomforts, or the leak in the plumbing at home. The Bible lesson has to compete with television, magazines, newspapers, movies, athletic events, family plans, and all the affairs of the workaday world. At the beginning of the class period the teacher must find a way to reach out, grab the learner by the lapels, and haul him or her into the lesson.

Some call it "creating learning readiness." Others refer to it as "motivating the learner." Educators speak of "establishing set." Whatever you call it, this is a crucial step in the lesson plan. If you don't get the learner's attention and interest at the start, you might as well forget the rest.

There are proven techniques for doing this. You can appeal to the learner's curiosity, for instance. Curiosity is a universal human characteristic, a powerful motivator in learning situations. Curiosity is that strong human tendency to seek answers to questions, solve riddles, search out the unknown, explore mysteries, and close gaps in knowledge.

An effective tool for unlocking the curiosity of learners is a well-phrased question. "When did David love an enemy so much that he almost lost the loyalty of his friends?" "Jesus said that everyone who looks at a woman lustfully has already committed adultery with her in his heart. Does this mean that one who actually commits adultery is no more guilty in God's eyes than one who lusts in his heart?" "How do you explain the apparent conflict between the Commandment, 'Honor thy father and mother,' and the saying of Jesus, 'If anyone comes to me and does not hate his own father and mother . . . he cannot be my disciple'?" Questions like these are bound to elicit responses from class members, at least from those who are still breathing.

You might even start off with a brief quiz. "Match the husbands and wives in the following list of biblical men and women: Abram, Milcah, Rebekah, Sarai, Nahor, Noah, Bethuel, Isaac, Jacob, Laban, Rachel." (Some of the names don't match.)

Involve members in a creative activity. At the beginning of a lesson emphasizing the nature of God, a teacher handed a bit of modeling clay and a sheet of paper to each member and said, "I want you to fashion something, or draw something, which symbolizes your conception of God." One person molded the clay into a figure "1" and explained, "The Lord our God is one Lord." Another drew clouds on the sheet of paper and said, "God is clothed in mystery. We can never fully know what God is like until we see him face to face." The class members became absorbed not only in their own creative efforts, but, also, in the ideas of other members.

Use audiovisuals to focus attention. One of the most gripping introductions to a Bible study I have ever seen was a filmstrip entitled, *The Creation,* a combination of striking photography and effective narration set to a beautiful musical background. When it was over, everyone in the class was ready to plunge into a study of the Genesis story of creation.

Attention-getting techniques are limited only by the scope of one's imagination. One teacher introduced a lesson on the parable of the sower by flinging a handful of seeds across the floor and asking follow-up questions: "Will these seeds grow?" "Why not?" "What conditions would cause them to grow?" In another class, as members filed in they found real tombstones cut from poster board and were asked to write their own epitaph.

Just one word of caution. I have described this part of the lesson plan as finding a way to "reach out, grab the learner by the lapels, and haul him or her into the lesson." Don't forget the last part of that statement. Some introductions can get the attention of learners but will not lead them into the lesson. I remember with some amusement a class session in which the teacher introduced a subject that proved to be terribly exciting to the crowd of teenagers there. (It had something to do with the social behavior of high schoolers.) They threw themselves into a lively, sometimes heated, discussion. But when the teacher tried to get into the Bible study, they wouldn't quit. They went on and on, and were still immersed in this "introductory" discussion when the period ended. Remember, the introduction must not only stop the learner in his tracks; it must also point him in the right direction.

TEACHING LAB ACTIVITY NO. 21

Instructions: Coming up with interesting introductions to lessons week after week calls for truly creative thinking. Creative thinking is just the opposite of "thinking in the same old way." In creative thinking you try to leap out of the familiar rut.

In this lab activity I want you to get a piece of paper and list at least ten different ways to begin a lesson. Assume that the lesson is based on the sixth chapter of Daniel, the passage mentioned earlier.

Avoid the attitudes which dampen creative thinking. Don't stop to evaluate your ideas; just put them down. Don't tell yourself, "Oh, that will never do." That's a sure way to get back into the rut. Ready? OK. Start listing ways to get learners interested in a lesson on Daniel 6, and don't stop before you have listed ten.

Don't read any further until you have finished your ten lesson introductions.

If you have finished, compare your ideas with these:

1. Present some striking information about lions, with gruesome details about their power, their ability to mutilate enemies, and their eating habits.

2. Ask class members to name some of the most terrible methods of execution they know of; ask what they would think of seeing a victim thrown into a pit filled with vicious lions.

3. Start with this statement: "There probably are many things associated with religion that we would not die to defend; but, presumably, there are some things related to your personal faith that are important enough to die for. What are those things?"

4. Ask the question: Why was Daniel thrown into the lion's den?

5. Say: "You have heard the expression, 'the law of the Medes and the Persians.' Where did this expression originate and what does it mean?"

6. Show part of a filmstrip which portrays this episode in the life of Daniel.

7. Have class sing the song, "Dare to Be a Daniel."

8. Carry a portable recorder (or just a microphone)

into class and lead a man-on-the-street interview with a class member playing the role of a bystander who witnessed the release of Daniel from the lion's den.

9. Have a member give a report on Darius, king of Babylon, whose decree caused Daniel to be thrown to the lions.

10. Start with a word-association test. Read a series of words and let members write down the first word that comes to mind after each is given. Use these words: Ham, black, night, mickey, Daniel.

Introducing Bible study activities. The introduction is the lesson's showcase. But you'll also want to have something in the stockroom. As important as the introduction is, Bible study activities constitute the heart of the lesson plan.

Bible study activities are numerous and varied. But, of course, you can actually use only those that you know about. Psychologists toss around a story about a small boy who always colored his kindergarten pictures black. He colored trees, flowers, rivers, houses, and even the sky black. Suspecting that the little boy had some deep-seated personality problem, a child psychologist had an interview with him. "Why do you color everything black?" the psychologist asked. "Because," said the lad, "I only have a black color crayon." Maybe you have noticed that some teachers color everything "lecture." It could be that they have no other colors in their box of learning activities.

Since we will take up teaching-learning methods more extensively in chapter 8, I won't deal with specific Bible study activities here (except by way of illustration). Rather, I want to suggest some guidelines to follow when developing this part of your lesson plan.

1. *Learning activities should fit purposes.*

If I wanted to teach a six-year-old how to ride a bicycle, I certainly wouldn't sit him down and lecture to him on "The History of the Bicycle." If my purpose were to help a teenager develop a love for the Bible, I wouldn't go about it by reciting the history of the divided kingdoms of Israel. But if I really did want him to memorize the names of the rulers of southern and northern Israel, I hardly think it would be worthwhile to show filmstrips on the subject. The Bible study activities which go into your lesson plan should be carefully fitted to the purposes which they are supposed to achieve.

To illustrate, look again at the lesson plan based on Daniel 6. When I devised that lesson plan, I had in mind a goal which was related to attitudes rather than to factual knowledge. I wanted class members to be inspired by Daniel's courageous example to take similarly courageous stands in the face of challenges to their own faith. I would not expect a single lesson to turn my class members into a band of Daniels, of course. But I would hope that this lesson would start them thinking about the areas in life where faithfulness to God is important. That would be a good beginning.

With a goal related to affective learning, I turned to activities which affect attitudes. Group discussion is such an activity, provided that the questions for discussion are designed to probe attitudes. The first and last questions in the lesson plan on Daniel 6 are good illustrations.

But suppose I had been thinking of a different kind of teaching-learning goal, a goal that called for factual learning. The Bible study activities in my lesson plan would have been quite different. I would have used methods like these:

• Ask selected class members to prepare reports on Darius, the "laws of the Medes and the Persians," and ancient

Babylon, with special emphasis on unfamiliar terms, such as "satraps." Let these reports be presented in a symposium.

• Have members, perhaps in study teams of two, prepare an outline of the events in this chapter.

• Lecture on the historical setting of the book of Daniel, using a map and a dateline showing this Babylonian captivity in relationship to other Old Testament captivities.

2. Learning activities must fit the available time.

In church settings, Bible teaching is often a struggle against time. When teachers get together to talk about their mutual problems, one almost always hears the familiar complaint, "I never seem to have enough time to finish the lesson." Some teachers unconsciously act out their nervousness about time pressures. I was in a class once where the teacher glanced anxiously at his watch whenever anyone asked an unscheduled question. It was his way of saying, "We really don't have time to talk about that if we're going to finish the lesson." Trying to do too much in too little time, teachers either race through the study session at breakneck speed, or leave the last part of the lesson dangling when the bell rings.

Since time is usually in short supply in Bible-study sessions, a teacher must plan learning activities with one eye on the clock. It makes no sense to include a twenty-six-minute film in your lesson if you have only eighteen minutes for it. And it doesn't pay to lead a group discussion if it must be rushed too much. A student once turned in a lesson plan in which he had allowed five minutes for "group discussion" in a class of fifteen. Assuming that everybody had at least one contribution to make to the discussion, that would be about thirty-three seconds per person.

When you are working on a lesson plan, it is good practice to estimate the time required for each activity. Then if your time estimates exceed the total time available, you can always cut something out in the planning stages. That's much better than cutting something out in the middle of a class session.

3. *Learning activities should be suited to the abilities of learners.*

Have you ever seen a person in a Bible study group struggle to pronounce those difficult names in an Old Testament passage, with embarrassing results? Nobody likes to look stupid. But that's exactly how a person feels, stumbling through a Scripture passage while the teacher patronizingly coaches him on every hard word. Learning activities should always be geared to the knowledge level and the skills of learners.

Bible-searching is an excellent learning technique. It can be an illuminating experience, for instance, to explore the numerous Scriptures pertaining to "the Word" in John 1:1-18. But class members must be trained to do this sort of thing. It requires familiarity with the books of the Bible and the ability to use concordances, Bible dictionaries, and center-column references.

Some learning activities are not so demanding from the standpoint of knowledge and skill, but they require a higher level of participation than learners are willing to accept. Many members of Bible study groups are so habituated to sitting primly in nice straight rows that they can't bear the thought of moving around a bit or expending energy in study activities. I knew a teacher of a men's Bible class in Louisville who, in order to encourage more participation in class discussions, arranged the chairs in his classroom in one large circle. This, of course, provided a front-row seat for everybody. Two of the back row types in his class were so upset by the new arrangement that they vowed not to return to class until the chairs had been "put back like they're supposed to be." Not everyone is that resistant to participation. But the teacher must be careful not to draw learners into learning activities which are too threatening for them.

Role play is a good case in point. In role play, individuals assume the identities of persons in some human conflict situation (a husband-wife quarrel, for instance) and act out the situation spontaneously. It's a good learning device, but some persons are just too shy to be thrust into such an activity.

I'm not suggesting that a teacher should always "play it safe," never involving class members in new approaches to learning. That's the road to dull monotony. The trick is to push learners as far as they are willing to venture into new study experiences, but no further. You usually know instinctively what level of involvement a group of learners will accept. So, in selecting study procedures, you use a "transformer technique," stepping the intensity of involvement upward or downward to the level of your class members.

Let's say that I am preparing to lead a study of Acts 1:1-11, with special emphasis on verse 8, "and you shall be my witnesses." You don't make witnesses of people by pointing a finger at them and saying, "Start witnessing!" A good starting place is to encourage Christians to tell about their own experience in Christ. Role play is an effective technique for doing this in class. I could organize class members into teams of three. One person would play the role of a non-Christian work associate. The second person, playing himself, would share his Christian testimony with the work associate. The third person in the team would act as an observer, evaluating the dialogue between the other two.

But, wait. Several of the men in the class won't be up to this; they'll feel that they have really been put on the spot. Maybe it would be less threatening to ask them to discuss their Christian experiences in small discussion groups of five or six. This would put their responses on a voluntary basis.

If I wanted to step down the intensity of involvement even more, I could give each member a letter from a hypothetical friend or relative asking him how and why he became a Christian. Then I would ask everybody to write a letter in response and bring it to class the following week. Having time to think about a reply should make it less difficult than responding on the spur of the moment.

You see the point I'm making. You can deal with the same material in class in different ways, some more difficult than others. The teacher should select study activities which won't get learners in over their heads.

There is another side to this, though. It's equally undesirable to operate below the level of class members. A teacher who tries to spoon-feed learners who are knowledgeable and capable, learners who are eager for involvement, will soon smother them with boredom.

4. Use variety in selecting learning activities.

Where the opportunity presents itself, an occasional change of pace from one kind of learning activity to another adds interest to the lesson. "Variety is the spice of life," they say. And there is truth in the saying. Anybody who has ever been on a highly restricted diet knows what a blessing it is to have a variety of food at one's disposal. We rearrange furniture, repaper or repaint walls, and change the color of the living room draperies all because variety makes life more interesting. We don't like monotonous tasks which require us to perform a single operation repeatedly. Is there any reason to believe that learners prefer to repeat the same study activity over and over again?

In many classes, learners have been conditioned to participate in only one kind of activity—listening. They listen as the teacher explains the biblical text, relates a story or two for illustration, throws in assorted personal observations, and tells how the lesson should be applied to life. Bible-searching assignments, group discussions, assigned reports, creative activities, pencil-and-paper exercises, role play, and question-and-answer periods can do much to break the monotony of a "sit-'em-down-and-tell-'em" approach.

Clinching the lesson. "Clinch" might not be a dignified word, but it expresses exactly what I want to say about the third function of the lesson plan. It means "to fix securely, make fast, rivet." You get the attention of the learners, lead them through planned learning experiences, then quick-freeze the learning before it has a chance to melt away. The quick-freezing process is what we are talking about here.

This part of the lesson plan is often spoken of as "applying the lesson to life." But that isn't relevant to every lesson. Sometimes one's teaching goal is strictly cognitive; the purpose being to help class members gain biblical knowledge which has little immediate application to life. How do you "apply" an understanding of apocalyptic literature to life? How do you relate information concerning the authorship of Hebrews to daily experience? There are many instances in which knowledge itself—not a real-life application of it—becomes the desired end-result of a lesson.

When you want class members to gain information, you clinch the lesson by reinforcing what they have learned. You can present a summary of the lesson, for instance. (This has been the purpose of the summary at the end of each chapter in this book.) Or let class members reconstruct outlines of the lesson.

Sometimes you might administer a brief quiz at the end of the period; or let learners, working in pairs, quiz each other. When time permits, you might even close the session with a contest between two teams (like an old-fashioned spelling bee), using questions based on the information in the lesson.

Sometimes, of course, your aim will be to get learning into life. When preparing to teach a lesson on the commissioning of the church's early missionaries in Acts 13, perhaps your aim will be to lead class members to commit themselves to more consistent support of missionary enterprises. Your goal for a lesson on Jesus' teachings concerning prayer in Matthew 6 and 7 might be to lead class members to establish the practice of prayer in their daily lives. With goals like this, you'll need something more than reviews and quizzes to "freeze" the results of the lesson.

I was leading a group of young married couples in a study of Matthew 6:19-34 on one occasion. To start the session, I asked each person to make a list of "the most important things in life." Then we combined these ideas into a master list. This list included such things as family, health, Christ, friends, intelligence, education, job, and home. Some were honest enough to mention money and other material possessions. Then I said, "Now I want you to imagine that you are going to have to give up all but five of these things. What would you give up first, and what would you keep at all costs? List the five things that you would keep." Toward the end of the session I referred to these lists again. "I want you to do one more thing," I said. "Rate the five things which you listed earlier, in terms of their permanency; that is to say, identify the things that you are most certain to have ten or twenty years from this date." The following week, one of our class members called me up and said, "I want you to know that what we did in class last Sunday made a deep impression on me. It made me realize that the things in life that are the most important to me are really the least durable. I've had to do a lot of thinking."

Putting Together a Lesson Plan

At this point, we've covered several things about lesson planning. But you might still have questions about actually putting a lesson plan together from beginning to end. So, being a firm believer in the power of demonstration, I want to present a complete lesson plan. Then, in separate notations, I'll explain my rationale for each step in the plan. As you read through it, keep in mind that the words in *italics* are used as explanatory notes. They are not part of the teaching plan itself.

A SAMPLE TEACHING PLAN

Bible Passages

Matt. 7:7-8; Jas. 5:16*b;* 2 Cor. 12:7-9; Matt. 26:39; Matt. 6:8

(Note: These Scriptures were designated as the passages for the lesson in a published curriculum. They all pertain to the theme of prayer. Generally speaking, I dislike studying the Bible in such a fragmentary fashion.)

Teaching Goals

At the end of this session, each learner should be able to: (1) name four purposes of prayer drawn from the Scriptures studied in this lesson, and (2) identify at least one purpose in prayer which needs greater emphasis in his or her life.

(Note: The first goal is mostly cognitive. The second has to do more with attitude, because the learner must make this choice on the basis of what he feels about his prayer life. Notice the two action verbs, "name" and "identify.")

Getting Attention

Ask class members to respond to the following true-false items. These are to be printed on large sheets of paper and taped to the wall, one by one. Each person will write responses on a slip of paper.

1. Whatever you ask in prayer, truly believing, you will receive.

2. According to the Bible, the prayers of a righteous man are always answered.

3. Because Paul was a righteous man, he always received what he prayed for.

4. Jesus was the only man who ever lived whose prayers were always answered.

5. One purpose of prayer is to let your needs be made known to God. (This should take no more than 5 minutes.)

(Note: Curiosity is a powerful motivator in learning situations. The true-false items are purposely designed to create uncertainty in the minds of learners. I am counting on this to stimulate their interest in the lesson.)

Bible Study Activities

1. Organize class members into groups of four. Let them compare their responses to the true-false items. Then display another large sheet of paper with the following Scripture references: Matthew 7:7-8; James 5:16*b;* 2 Corinthians 12:7-9; Matthew 26:39; Matthew 6:8. Ask the members of each group to reconsider their responses to the true-false items in light of these Scriptures and to try to come to an agreement on the correct answers. (Allow about 15 minutes for this.)

(Note: The groups of four will provide a setting in which each individual can "try out" his responses on others. This will lead to discussion of principles related to prayer. The discussion should be lively, since there will be disagreement on the correct answers to the true-false items. Notice that the Scripture references are presented in such a way that

class members will have to locate them in their own Bibles. It's important, in Bible study, for people to actually handle the Scriptures. Take time to read each of these Scriptures and you will see that they are likely to create even more uncertainty about the responses to the true-false items. The purpose of this is to motivate the learners to try to resolve the questions in their minds.

2. Lead a large-group discussion of these Bible passages, taking into account the responses to the true-false items. Use these questions to stimulate discussion: (1) Should Matthew 7:7-8 be taken literally? (2) James 5:16*b* suggests that the prayers of Christians might have powerful effects. What effects might be expected from prayer? (3) What good came of Paul's prayers concerning the "thorn in the flesh"? (4) If Jesus knew that the cross was inescapable, why did he pray, "let this cup pass from me"? (5) If God knows our needs even before we pray, why voice our needs in prayer? (Allow 15 minutes for this discussion.)

(Note: In addition to clarifying the meaning of the Bible passages, this large-group discussion will provide an opportunity for "cross-fertilization" of ideas which, up to this point, have been confined to small groups.

3. In a brainstorming session, have members give as many answers as possible to the question: "What are the purposes of prayer?" Write their answers on the chalkboard. (This should take 5 minutes.)

(Note: This brainstorming process is designed to stimulate ideas for the steps to follow. During this process, some will mention purposes in prayer that will not have occurred to others. Thus, learners will teach learners.

Clinching the Lesson

1. Ask each person to write down the four purposes of prayer that are most important in his or her own life, then

to rank them in the order of their importance. (Allow 3 minutes.)

(Note: This step will shift the emphasis from "What does the Bible say about prayer?" to the question, "Just where do I stand in relation to these teachings?" The ranking exercise is intended to encourage each person to do some serious thinking concerning his or her own prayer life.)

2. Ask each person to identify one purpose in prayer which needs more emphasis in his or her own prayer life. (Call attention to the list of purposes on the board.) (Allow 2 minutes.)

(Note: Learning involves change. Obviously the learners do not need to change what they are doing right. They need to identify weaknesses in their prayer lives. This exercise will encourage them to compare "what is" with "what ought to be."

In groups of four again, let each person take one minute to share with his or her group one of the responses given in the two activities above.

(Note: Public sharing of private decisions heightens commitment to them. The reason for asking learners to share only one of the responses is that this will let them decide whether to share a strength or weakness.)

Time to Summarize

In this chapter we have discussed the development of a blueprint for leading a class session. A lesson plan is an outline of teaching procedures, an action strategy, not an outline of the content of the lesson.

The lesson plan should (1) tell how the teacher intends to get the attention of class members so as to draw them into the lesson; (2) describe the Bible-study activities which are to be used in the session; and (3) indicate how the teacher purposes to "clinch" the lesson.

An excellent way to engage the interest of learners is to stimulate curiosity by asking questions, posing dilemmas, or presenting problems to be solved. Creative activities and audiovisuals also are good for stimulating interest. The introduction to a lesson should do more than get attention, however; it should also lead learners into the lesson material.

Bible-study activities constitute the heart of the lesson plan. A wide variety of teaching-learning techniques lies at the disposal of a teacher who will learn how to use them. And it's important to become familiar with as many methods as possible. Using the same approach to Bible study all the time is something like playing on a piano that has only one key.

In planning study activities, the teacher should be guided by the following principles:

• Learning activities should fit purposes.
• Learning activities must fit the available time.
• Learning activities should be suited to the abilities of learners.
• Use variety in selecting learning activities.

"Clinching" the lesson means fixing it securely in the minds and lives of learners. When the lesson is designed to help them gain knowledge, this can take the form of summarizing or reviewing the material. When the teacher's aim is to "get the learning into life," clinching the lesson means finding ways to bridge the gap between hearing the Word and doing it.

It would seem appropriate at this juncture to present a teaching lab activity which would call on you to prepare a lesson plan, since that has been the subject of this chapter. But we will postpone that experience for the time being, since the next two chapters will also have an important bearing on the preparation of lesson plans.

7
Speaking of Methods

I once wrote an article on teaching methods that didn't set very well with one reader. "That's just the trouble with our public schools today," he wrote, "all this emphasis on methods. In Bible teaching we need to forget about methods and concentrate on content."

Forget about methods? That might have sounded a little strange to the Master Teacher. No, I'm not suggesting that he spoke of "educational methodology" as we do today. But he certainly used a variety of methods in his own teaching. He "concentrated on content." But he communicated that content in many different ways.

How incredible it was for a rabbi to wash the feet of his disciples! (John 13:1-14). But Jesus wasn't just getting feet clean. He was teaching his followers an unforgetable lesson. We learn the "content" of that lesson in verse 14: "If I then, your Lord and Teacher, have washed your feet, you also ought to wash one another's feet" (RSV). But why did Jesus go to so much trouble to get that truth across? Why didn't he "forget about methods," and just come out and say it? ("Men, I want you to be willing to serve one another.") Because he knew the power of a living example. He even lets us know that his choice of method was deliberate, calculated to produce a desired effect: "For I have given you an example, that you also should do as I have done to you" (John 13:15, RSV).

On an earlier occasion, when Jesus asked someone for a

coin and asked, "Whose likeness and inscription is this?" he was teaching an object lesson. Why did he go to all this trouble? Why didn't he simply say, "Render to Caesar the things that are Caesar's, and to God the things that are God's"? (Mark 12:17, RSV). Because he knew the power of a teaching method.

When Jesus fed the multitude by the Sea of Tiberius (John 6:1-13), he wasn't merely filling hungry stomachs. He was teaching a lesson by way of demonstration. The "content" of the lesson was, "I am the bread of life." But he taught it in an unforgettable way.

He was a master of storytelling, an ancient teaching method which is just as effective today. He often used questions to lead his pupils into new vistas of truth. And he was adept at using visual illustrations to drive home his points.

Any teacher must be concerned about method; because methods are the tools of the trade. A surgeon has his instruments, an artist his brushes, a carpenter his tools, and a teacher his methods. Just as each instrument, brush, and tool is designed to achieve a specific purpose, so is each teaching method. And part of the teacher's skill (as in the case of surgeons, artists, and carpenters) is to be able to select the right tool for a given job.

Ways of Looking at Methods

One time I decided to impress a class with the sheer number of teaching methods available. I ended up impressing myself. I started listing all the methods I knew on a long roll of wrapping paper, and when I finished I had a list of methods which reached all the way down a nine-foot wall and, then, six feet across the floor.

With so many methods available, how does one get to know them, much less learn how to use them? I have two suggestions. First, you learn to think about methods in terms of their purposes. Second, you don't try to learn all of them at once; you first master the teaching methods which you are likely to use most.

Think again of a carpenter's tools. They have different purposes. Hammers are for striking things forcibly. Saws, knives, and chisels are for cutting. Clamps are for holding, rulers for measuring. That's what I mean by classifying methods in terms of their purposes. To carry the comparison further, even though many specialized tools are available, a carpenter probably uses hammer, square, ruler, and saw more than any other tools. It stands to reason that he should master those tools first. Some teaching methods are just that basic; as basic as the carpenter's hammer, square, ruler, and saw. We will look at three of these later. But, just now, let's consider some ways of looking at methods in terms of their purposes.

Exposition and inquiry. Ted Smith and Marge Jones both taught lessons on the theme of worship based on Isaiah 6. Ted presented a carefully prepared lecture. His outline included these points:

    I. A Vision of God (6:1-4)
   II. Confession of Sin (6:5)
  III. Cleansing from Sin (6:6-7)
  IV. Call to Service (6:8*a*)
   V. Responding to the Call (6:8*b*)

After the lesson, several members of the class told Ted that they had gotten a lot out of the lesson.

Marge took a different approach. She asked the women in her class to study Isaiah 6, noting carefully the elements of the prophet's unusual worship experience. The women worked in study teams of three. They had a number of commentaries on Isaiah available on a nearby table. After a twenty-minute study period, Marge asked them to report what they had found out. She wrote their findings on the chalkboard. Then, guided by suggestions from the class she compiled an outline on the chalkboard under the title, "Elements of a Worship Experience." The outline looked like this:

I. Worship begins with a sense of God's presence and with praise.

II. A sense of God's presence leads to confession of sin.

III. Confession of sin results in a sense of God's forgiveness.

IV. The worshiper feels God's call.

V. True worship leads one to answer God's call.

Finally, working in the same study teams of three, Marge's class members outlined sample worship services, including specific Scripture readings and hymns, following the outline above.

The two classes studied the same Scripture passage. They even covered essentially the same points. But the two classes were different. Ted's lesson focused on this presentation; Marge's lesson focused on an experience of discovery. Ted studied the Scripture passage and shared his findings with the class; Marge, too, studied the Scripture passage, but her approach was to lead class members to find out for themselves what was in it. Ted was active; his class members were receptive. Both Marge and her class members were active participants in the study session.

Educators have names for these two different approaches to teaching. What Ted did is called "exposition." This word comes from a Latin word which means "to put out" or "to set forth." And that is what Ted was doing. He was "putting out information," or "setting forth ideas."

Marge's approach is known as "inquiry" teaching, because,

in this kind of teaching, the learners conduct an inquiry into the subject matter. "Inquiry" comes from a Latin word which means "seek into." Marge led her class to "seek into the passage of Scripture" to see what they could find out about it.

The unspoken assumption underlying expository teaching is that the teacher alone has information worth sharing with the class. The assumption implicit in inquiry teaching is that class members are capable of discovering worthwhile truths.

Which is the best approach, expository teaching or inquiry teaching? It depends upon what you are trying to accomplish. If you want to cover a lot of information in the shortest possible time, better stick to exposition. But if you want class members to learn how to explore Scripture for themselves or develop their own insights into the meaning of Bible passages, inquiry teaching would be the preferred approach.

Some methods seem to lend themselves to expository teaching, while others are more harmonious with inquiry teaching. For instance, lecturing, calling on learners to recite factual information, presenting information by filmstrip or recording, or giving quizzes on assigned readings would fall into the category of expository teaching. On the other hand, group discussion, problem-solving, case studies, role playing, and creative activities would generally be classified as inquiry teaching.

TEACHING LAB ACTIVITY NO. 22

Instructions: Below you will find brief descriptions of various teaching procedures. Indicate which ones you think are examples of "expository teaching" by writing "EX" in front of them. Identify the procedures which you think are examples of "inquiry teaching" by writing "IN" in front of them.

_____ The teacher said, "When Paul went to new cities on his first missionary journey, he often went to the Jewish synagogues. Why do you think he did this?" Then she gave the learners five minutes to discuss this question before reporting their answers.

_____ The teacher asked class members to write an imaginary constitution and bylaws for a new church in Asia Minor during the first century.

_____ The teacher presented a filmstrip, *Principles of Bible Interpretation,* then gave a brief quiz on its content.

_____ The teacher distributed a written case study which told the story of a man who had to decide whether or not to shoot an intruder in order to protect his family. Then class members were instructed to decide what they would do in light of the meaning of the Sixth Commandment.

_____ The teacher presented a really interesting lecture on the geography of Palestine.

_____ Class members were asked to put themselves in the place of Abraham and to write a diary entry about his feelings (1) when he was first instructed to sacrifice Isaac and (2) when he came down from the mountain after Isaac had been spared.

_____ The teacher instructed class members to find the names of three women of questionable morality in the genealogy in Matthew 1.

Don't read any further until you have filled in all the blanks above.

If you are working with a group, or with a study partner, compare your answers with theirs.

(Here are my answers to the items above: IN, IN, EX, IN, EX, IN, IN.)

Cognitive and affective learning. In the discussion of "cognitive" and "affective" learning goals in chapter 5, I indicated that some teaching methods were better for achieving cognitive learning and others for affective learning. I don't want to push this distinction too far, since some methods seem to be able to achieve both kinds of results. A stirring lecture, for instance, can produce changes in attitude as well as changes in knowledge. And group discussion can produce both cognitive and affective learning, depending on how it is handled. But, generally speaking, these two kinds of learning call for different teaching approaches.

Cognitive learning takes place through teaching methods which stimulate thinking, remembering, evaluating, and reasoning. Let's look at some samples of methods like this.

If you want learners to memorize information or learn material well enough to recall it, you employ methods which emphasize drill and review. To illustrate, if I wanted to help class members memorize Psalm 100, I would write one verse at a time on the board. I would have the class repeat a verse three times, then erase a few key words and see if they could still repeat the verse. If they could, I would go on to erase a few more words and have them repeat the verse again until, finally, they could recite the whole verse without having any of the words before them.

If you want learners to grasp a new concept, an effective way to accomplish that is to state the concept, then give examples to illustrate it. Consider the concept of "signs" in the Gospel of John. A sign was a miracle, but not just a miracle. A sign always conveyed some significant truth about Jesus. You might say that a sign was a teaching miracle. The first sign was the miracle at the wedding feast at Cana (John 2:11). The circumstances of this miracle, the changing of water into wine, suggested that Jesus had come to fulfill what was lacking in the old Judaism. (We can't go into that here, but the passage makes for interesting study.) Another sign was the "feeding of the five thousand" (John 6:14). It conveyed the truth that Jesus was the "bread of life" (6:35). Yet another sign, the raising of Lazarus (John 11:1-44), taught that Jesus was "the resurrection and the life" (11:25). You see, a sign was not just a miraculous act; a sign always taught an important theological truth.

In the preceding paragraph, I did just what I suggested at the beginning of it. I stated a concept, the meaning of the term "sign" in John, then provided examples to illustrate it.

You will often attempt to help class members understand the meaning of some passage of Scripture which might be a bit difficult to grasp. "Paraphrasing" is a good technique to use for such a purpose. To paraphrase a passage of Scripture, you simply restate it in your own words in a way which conserves its meaning. A paraphrase of Ephesians 2:14-16 might look like this: "Although there used to be a huge chasm between Jews and Gentiles, Jesus has brought us together. It isn't that he just made the two camps compatible; he has actually made one camp out of the two. There aren't two camps anymore. Christ has done this by the power of the cross. One can't come to the foot of the cross without drawing near to other people who are there. And they include both Jews and Gentiles."

Without looking at it, could you list all the separate petitions contained in the Lord's Prayer? If you were a member of my class, and I had adopted this as a teaching goal, I probably would ask you to do some pencil-and-paper work for a few minutes, breaking that prayer (in Matt. 6:9-13) down into its various parts. This is an example of another kind of cognitive learning, sometimes called analysis. After you had completed your analysis of the Lord's Prayer, the next step in a classroom situation would be to let you and other learners compare the results of your work.

Now, let's turn to some illustrations of the kinds of methods which lend themselves to affective learning. Remember that affective learning has to do with attitudes. And we learn attitudes primarily from other people; they just sort of rub off on us.

I never have enjoyed meeting snakes in their natural habitat—or anywhere else, for that matter. An unexpected confrontation with a wriggling reptile, even a small, nonpoisonous one, can send chills up and down my spinal column and make my feet want to make tracks—fast. Now, that isn't logical. There's no rational excuse for fearing all kinds of reptiles, including some which are quite harmless. But, you see, I didn't learn this attitude through any rational process. I "caught" it from someone else who feared snakes.

Bobbie (my wife) is that way about windy weather. She doesn't panic, exactly, but she always feels uneasy when we have a thunderstorm or gusty winds. Why? Because she grew up in a part of the country where tornadoes are always a threat, and in her childhood she spent many a stormy night sitting in the dark shadows of a storm cellar with her family. Her parents were uneasy about storms; she caught that attitude.

We also catch more positive attitudes from those around us. Since I have already used Bobbie's experience as an illustration, maybe she won't mind my referring to her again. One of the things I like about my wife is her love for gardening. Some people go to their "shrink" when things get tense; Bobbie goes to her garden. She goes out in her grubby jeans and faithful old sweatshirt and works in the soil. It always has a therapeutic effect. Where did she pick up such a positive attitude toward an activity which some folks look upon as sheer drudgery? No question about it. She caught it from her mother. As a little girl, she spent many a happy hour working at her mother's side in the family garden. And you want to know something else? Over the years, I finally caught it from Bobbie.

This same principle works in the area of religious attitudes. From her mother my wife also inherited an unquestioning faith in the power of prayer. When life gets too heavy, pray about it. When the burdens multiply, take them to the Lord in prayer. When the way is unclear, ask the Spirit for guidance. That's the way it always is with her; as natural as breathing. And I know that this came about through living with a mother who was a great person of prayer.

If we "catch" attitudes from persons, it stands to reason that affective learning is achieved through methods which are highly personal in nature. Certain kinds of group discussion are like this. I say "certain kinds" because some group discussions place more emphasis on information and ideas than on personal experience. A discussion of the topic, "The Role of the Judges in the History of Israel," would be a content-centered discussion. But a discussion of a topic like, "The Role of Prayer in My Life as a Christian," would be a person-centered discussion, because the participants would be talking about themselves rather than about things outside themselves. Person-centered discussion groups can often bring about changes in attitudes and feelings.

Have you noticed how some motion-picture films can involve a person emotionally? That's because films have the power to draw us into the picture, so to speak. We put ourselves into the shoes of characters in the film; our emotions resonate with their feelings. Thus, for a brief time, we vicariously experience the excitement of adventure, the pangs of sorrow, the warm glow of love, along with the people in the film.

Interestingly, personal stories on the printed page have a similar effect. Many a Christian in recent years has been caught up in the story of Corrie Ten Boom, who struggled so valiantly to maintain a glowing Christian faith through long years of persecution at the hands of the Nazis. It's hard to read through one of her books without having your own faith lifted and your desire to be a faithful disciple strengthened.

Translated into teaching methodology, this means that the teacher who wishes to bring about attitudinal learning will consider using testimonies, case studies, films, recordings, stories, dramatizations, and reading material which focuses on personal experience.

Don't underestimate the power of music in the emotional and attitudinal realm. Lives there a Frenchman whose patriotic fervor is not quickened by the strains of the *Marseillaise*, or an Englishman whose heart is not warmed by the singing of *God Save Our Queen?* And, in spite of the critics who insist that our national anthem isn't good music, many Americans still feel a tingle of pride and gratitude when a band strikes up the *Star-Spangled Banner.*

Think of the emotional appeal of hymns and gospel songs. What more fitting way to close a study session designed to heighten devotion to the Christ of the cross and inspire allegiance to the way of the cross than to play a recording of Isaac Watts's great hymn, "When I Survey the Wondrous Cross," during a period of silent meditation?

Role playing is another powerful technique for exploring attitudes. Picture a women's Bible class engaged in a study of the story of the woman caught in the act of adultery in John 8:2-11. The teacher asks two class members to role-play a situation in which one is a seventeen-year-old girl whose best friend has just discovered that she is pregnant. The other class member plays the role of the girl's mother. The daughter is trying to convince her mother that there is no harm in continuing to double-date with her friend, still unmarried, and her boyfriend. The mother has doubts. After the role play has gone on for two or three minutes, the teacher stops the action and asks the class to talk about how they would have handled this situation.

There is another technique, sometimes referred to as "creative writing," which can be useful for exploring attitudes. A friend of mine used this approach during a lesson on the Scripture passage mentioned above, John 8:2-11. He instructed the young adults in his class to write a personal letter or a poem depicting the feelings of one of the persons at the scene—the adulterous woman, Jesus, or one of the scribes and Pharisees who dragged the woman into the presence of Jesus. A poem written by one of the young women in the class was electrifying. She had tried to portray the inner experience of the adultress, and had done so with unusual perception and poignancy. A hushed silence settled over the room as she shared what she had written. Later, my friend commented on this experience to someone after class, and was told: "The story of the woman in the Bible passage was the story of the young woman in your class before she became a Christian."

Mastering Basic Tools

At the very beginning, I shared with you some of the basic convictions that have shaped this book. One of those convictions is that a teacher must master the basic tools of teaching, the "bread and butter" methods, before tinkering with more innovative approaches. Once in a while I come across a would-be teacher who is like a cook who fixes fancy desserts but doesn't know how to prepare vegetables, bake breads, or turn meats into edible dishes; he's great on "creative activities," but doesn't know how to deliver a lecture or keep a group discussion on track. I am a firm believer in the educational value of creative activities, rightly used. But people can't live on desserts all the time.

So what I propose to do in this section is to describe three fundamental teaching methods, methods on which you will rely most heavily. And I want to share some practical suggestions for using these methods effectively.

Lecture. Let's begin with one of the oldest and one of the most controversial teaching methods around today, the lecture. Why controversial? Well, it still holds the honor of being the most widely used teaching method in education today. And it probably is used in Bible teaching more than any other method. But, on the other hand, many people have developed an intense dislike for the lecture method, probably because they spent so many years in classrooms being bored to the extreme by bad lecturing. They regard the lecture with disdain. They pronounce the very word *lecture* with a sneer. They use unflattering clichés to describe lecturing, such as "sit still while I instill." And some express serious doubt that anything can be learned by listening to lectures. "Teaching isn't telling," they say. But that point of view doesn't find much support in educational research. I, too, have doubts about the tendency of many teachers to overuse the lecture method. And I, too, have squirmed in my seat through endless hours of poor lecturing. But, we might as well face it, lecture is going to be around for sometime to come. And teachers will continue to use it. That being the case, the smart thing to do is to learn to use it well.

Lecture is formally defined as "informative discourse before an audience." The use of a lecture assumes that the teacher has something which learners need to hear or want to hear, something worth sharing. It also helps if the teacher knows how to share it well. And that is what the following suggestions are all about.

1. Know what you are talking about.

When you lecture, become familiar with your subject. Do enough background study to make the material a part of your thinking. A lecture is not a patchwork quilt of random ideas and choice quotations hastily thrown together and casually delivered. If it's worth lecturing about, it's worth learning about.

2. Use lecture in combination with other methods.

One reason for the unpopularity of lecturing in some quarters is that many teachers use it to the exclusion of all other approaches. No teaching method is that good. The ear of the learner can take in just so much information. What the lecturer says needs to be supported by visuals—outlines, diagrams, graphic illustrations. Rather than merely talk about the ten cities of the Decapolis—use a classroom map to show where this region was located in New Testament times. Instead of trying to describe, in words alone, the Temple area in Jerusalem where Paul got into trouble (Acts 21:28), use a model or a sketch of the Temple to illustrate the point.

Don't lecture for more than ten minutes at a time without having the class do something else, as a change of pace. Ask a question, and pause long enough for responses. Have learners write something on a worksheet. Let them turn to the persons sitting next to them to discuss a point. Take a sampling of opinion, asking for a show of hands. Play a thirty-second excerpt from a recording. Have somone read a quotation from a book. There are many ways to break the lockstep cadence of a lecture, and at the same time reinforce what the lecturer has to say.

3. Focus and refocus attention.

Remember that there is a limit to the information processing capacity of human beings. They can't pay attention to too many things at once. If you use visuals or other learning devices in connection with a lecture, don't let these compete with what you are saying.

If you plan to display a written outline on the chalkboard or on a large sheet of paper, don't reveal the whole outline at once. Because, if you do, some class members will be so busy copying the outline that they won't hear what you are saying. While you are still on point two, they will be writing down point five. Use the "disclosure method" to reveal each point as you come to it. Simply cover all the points in the outline with strips of paper before you start, then peel them off point by point.

If you are fortunate enough to have an overhead projector, don't leave it on all the time you are talking, unless you happen to be referring to the projected image itself. When you want the class to look, turn on the projector; when you want them to listen to you, turn it off. Focus attention on a visual, then refocus attention on your lecture; but not both at the same time.

While learners search for a Scripture passage during an interlude in your lecture, don't keep on talking. Give them time to search, then resume your lecture after they have found the Scripture.

4. Make ample use of illustration.

One point at which we need to follow the example of the Master Teacher is in the abundant use of illustrations. It is hard for a learner to grasp a barrage of verbal statements without an occasional illustration to imbue them with concrete meaning.

Jesus was concerned about the way the gospel was "going in one ear and out the other" as some people listened to his teaching; so he told a story about a sower of seed, and talked about how the birds came and snatched up some of the seed as soon as it had fallen on the ground. He wanted his hearers to know how extremely important it was to seek the kingdom of God; so he told the story of a merchant who found one pearl which was so valuable to him that he sold everything else in order to buy it. Again and again, he communicated profound truth through everyday visual imagery.

Illustrations are the windows which open up the lecture to the understanding of the hearers. They don't always have to take the form of stories. A brief metaphor ("the tongue is a fire") can speak worlds of truth. A simple graphic design can support a significant concept.

Consider this one:

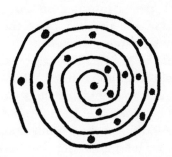

"Our doctrinal beliefs may be represented by the dots on this diagram. Some are on the outer fringe. We could give them up or exchange them for other beliefs without any great sense of loss. But, as we move toward the center, we find beliefs that grow increasingly important to us. And at the very center are those convictions for which we might even die. What about you? Which beliefs are out there on the fringes, and which are absolutely central to your faith?"

Question and Answer. So long as there are teachers and learners, questions will be used as educational tools. The method is older than Confucius. It was made famous by the Greek philosopher, Socrates. Jesus himself was a master of the art of asking penetrating questions. And questions continue to be used as a major educational tool in classrooms today.

In chapter 3 I suggested that questions should vary in form, scope, and difficulty, and talked about the differences between narrow and broad questions. Go back and review the examples in that discussion. Note, also, the word of caution concerning the use of yes-no questions. Then read the suggestions below concerning the different kinds of questions which you might wish to use in the classroom.

1. If you want specific information, ask specific questions.

The class is studying the history of the Old Testament patriarchs. They have been discussing the many evidences of faith in the life of Abram. Then the teacher asks, "What about Lot?" Well, what about him? What does the teacher want to know? Such an ambiguous question is likely to leave the class in silence, since they're not quite sure how to get a handle on it. If the teacher wants specific answers, he might ask, "Can we infer anything about Lot's religious faith from the crucial choice which he made when he parted ways with Abram?"

2. Express a concept, then ask learners for examples.

Paul once wrote, "The love of money is the root of all kinds of evil." Can you think of people in the Bible whose lives exemplify this truth?

This question requires recall of information; but, more than this, the learner must do some hard thinking about the meaning of that information. A question of this kind may be used when the teacher wishes to reinforce a biblical concept by the recitation of concrete examples.

Here is another example of this type of question: "God is depicted in the Old Testament as a God of wrath and judgment; but he is also portrayed as a God of love and mercy. Can you think of biblical situations in which both of these divine qualities are reflected in the same episode?

3. Ask hypothetical questions to stimulate discussion.

On occasion you will want to use questions based on purely imaginary circumstances in order to stimulate creative thinking and start discussions.

Here are some examples:

"Suppose you had been called upon to appear as defense attorney for Adam and Eve after they had eaten the forbidden fruit. What points might you have made in their behalf?"

"What if Saul of Tarsus had not been converted? In how many ways would subsequent Christian history have been different?"

"If John the Baptist were living today just as he lived during the earthly life of Jesus, would your church welcome him as a member?"

4. Pose problem-questions to stimulate thinking about certain biblical principles.

To kick off a study of the Eighth Commandment, "Thou shalt not steal," a teacher posed this question: "If you had no other way to get food for your children, would you steal?"

In connection with a study of the concluding chapter of 1 Thessalonians, this question was introduced: "In this passage we read, 'Abstain from all appearance of evil' (5:22). Yet, Jesus associated with people who were regarded as sinners. He was even accused of being a 'glutton and a drunkard, a friend of tax collectors and sinners' (Matt. 11:19, RSV). In light of this, how should we interpret this passage?"

These questions pose dilemmas. They are deliberately designed to produce uncertainty in the minds of learners, in order to provoke enough curiosity to lead learners into an exploration of the issues involved. When you introduce questions of this kind, you should have thought through your own position, but don't express your point of view too early in the discussion.

Group Discussion. Dull group discussion can be just as boring as dull lectures. And it sometimes happens that way. While almost everybody recognizes how important it is to prepare a lecture, there are some teachers who just assume that a group discussion will take care of itself; so they just go into class and say, "OK, let's discuss."

Group discussion is a vitally important teaching method, especially for the Bible teacher. Rarely should a Bible study session be conducted without group discussion in one form or another.

Here are a few principles which relate to the effective use of group discussion techniques:

1. Group size should vary according to the purpose.

The size of discussion groups can fluctuate between two and twelve, depending upon what you are trying to accomplish. Just two persons may team up to work on short problem-solving assignments in class. If the class is large, chairs hard to move, and time short, this is a quick way to get dialogue into the session. It requires a minimum of movement for class members to pair off in twos.

For person-centered discussions in which the participants talk about their attitudes, values, and experiences, groups of three or four are appropriate. This makes for an intimate grouping which is conducive to such discussion.

Five is about right for task-oriented groups. A task-oriented group is one which has a definite assignment to complete. For example, they might be asked, during a study of 1 and 2 Corinthians, to draw up some bylaws to deal with problems mentioned by the apostle Paul. When you have fewer than five in task-oriented groups, it is sometimes difficult to generate enough ideas within the groups. But when you have more than five, it is difficult for all the group members to "get into the act."

Groups of from six to twelve are about right for content-centered discussions (as opposed to person-centered discussions). A content-centered group is one which focuses on questions or issues such as, "What was Paul's attitude toward marriage?" If you have many more than twelve in such a group, members who are inclined to be shy and passive will tend not to say anything, because it's hard to "get a word in edgewise."

2. Give discussion groups specific assignments.

To say to a discussion group, "I want you to discuss what it means to be a Christian," is to make it likely that they will paddle around in a puddle of vague ideas for the allotted time. The question is too ambiguous. Groups should know clearly what they are supposed to be discussing. It's usually a good idea to give them assignments in writing. The following assignment would be an improvement on the one above: "You will have thirty minutes to discuss these three questions:

(1) What are the advantages of Christian discipleship?

(2) What are the disadvantages of Christian discipleship?

(3) What are the Christian's sources of power?"

3. Give task-oriented groups a chance to report.

If you have asked groups to solve problems, do research, answer questions, or come to conclusions, don't just leave the results of their discussions dangling. Give them an opportunity to share the fruits of their toil. There are two good reasons for doing so. First, group members tend to become discouraged if they feel that their group discussion had no significance. Second, where the class has been divided into groups, a report period gives the whole class a chance to pool ideas.

4. Provide essential resources.

If discussion groups are asked to talk about the meaning of a difficult passage of Scripture, they might need to consult commentaries. If you assign them the task of locating Bible references related to a particular doctrinal theme, they might have need of concordances. I have seen situations in which groups were asked to discuss a particular passage of Scripture, and there weren't enough Bibles in the groups for everyone to even look at the passage. Don't force discussion groups to make bricks without straw. Give them the needed materials to carry out your assignments.

5. Don't ask discussion groups to go beyond their level of knowledge.

Eight men sat in the classroom. The teacher divided them into two groups. "Group A will discuss the promise of the Holy Spirit," he explained. "Group B will discuss the power of the Spirit. I have extra Bibles if anybody needs one." Nothing happened. After about five minutes, several of the men were just gazing around the room.

The first problem was that the assignments were vague. The men didn't have any idea what they were supposed to be discussing. The second problem was that they weren't really all that familiar with Scriptures related to the promise and the power of the Holy Spirit. They just didn't have enough information. The discussions would have gone better had the teacher prepared them by telling them a week in advance what they would be discussing. Group discussion should not be a pooling of ignorance.

6. Group discussion is not a monologue.

Sounds silly to say that group discussion is not a monologue, doesn't it? Everybody knows that. Yet, I have known teachers to announce that they were going to "lead a discussion" of a certain topic in class, then spend the next forty minutes talking to the class.

It isn't easy for a teacher to resist the temptation to jump into a group discussion and dominate it. When two or more groups are going in the classroom, it is best for the teacher to observe from a distance.

Summary

In this chapter we have been doing just what the title suggests, "speaking of methods." We first considered two ways of classifying teaching methods. We found that some methods lend themselves to "expository" teaching, and others are better suited to "inquiry" teaching. Expository teaching magnifies the teacher's role as "presenter of information," while inquiry teaching emphasizes the learner's exploratory activity as he searches for knowledge.

Then we considered the two categories, "cognitive" and "affective" learning, as a way of looking at teaching methods. Methods which emphasize remembering, thinking, analyzing, and other mental activities are more conducive to cognitive learning. Methods which promote affective learning are person-centered.

We then focused on three basic teaching methods—lecture, question-and-answer, and group discussion. There are, of course many other teaching methods; so many, in fact, that it would take another volume to deal with them adequately, which is exactly the reason that they weren't treated in this chapter. (Books describing other methods are listed in the Appendix.)

Why have we focused in on just three methods? My point

of view is that a teacher who masters these three basic tools of the trade will be able to function in the classroom acceptably well. This doesn't mean, of course, that the teacher doesn't need to know other methods. One may be an adequate teacher with a knowledge of basic methods. But one becomes an excellent teacher as he or she masters a broad spectrum of educational methods.

8
How to Generate Enthusiasm for Bible Study

Fifty Bible teachers were busily engaged in conversation about their mutual joys and woes. As always, someone brought up the problem of nonparticipation in class. "My class members just don't seem to be interested in anything," a teacher said. "No matter what I do, they just sit there." Several others shared their own versions of the same problem. Finally, a soft-spoken little man sitting in the back of the room said, "I ought not to say anything, because I'm not a teacher. I came to this meeting with my wife. But I can tell you what's wrong with most of those class members you're talking about." He paused momentarily. "They're bored to death."

It was quite a bombshell to drop on a group of hardworking teachers. Everyone sat in stunned silence for several seconds. You could almost hear half-a-hundred teachers ask themselves, "Are my class members bored?"

One hot afternoon in July, I had a long talk over an ice-cream cone with four young adults who were terribly worried about their Bible class. At the beginning of the year their's had been a thriving class, filled with enthusiastic learners, attracting newcomers almost weekly. But they had changed teachers; and, soon, attendance had begun to decline. Now, three months later, only six or seven regulars were showing up each week. What had gone wrong?

"Our present teacher is a sincere person," they went on to say, "and he has our interests at heart. But our class sessions are just super dull. He does all the talking from beginning to end. No one else has a chance to say anything. We think we could make some suggestions that would make our class sessions more interesting, but we don't know how to tell him without hurting his feelings."

I'm not here to judge the teacher of that class. After all, I heard only one version of the story. Who knows what other factors might have influenced the situation? But it's a sad thing when—for whatever reason—Bible study becomes dull. We teach a vibrant, dynamic Word. It glows with exciting, life-changing truth. How is it possible to take this living Word and make it the basis of an exercise in dullness?

Fortunately, boredom in Bible study is neither inescapable nor incurable. Any teacher can take positive steps to generate enthusiasm for Bible study. That will be the focus of this chapter.

I have five suggestions:
- Build a spirit of fellowship.
- Personify enthusiasm.
- Get class members involved.
- Magnify persons.
- Use old-fashioned public relations.

These aren't offered as some kind of magic formula. They won't turn lethargic classes into buzzing dynamos at the drop of a hat. But they will offer guidance to the teacher who wants to put more vitality into Bible study.

Build a Spirit of Fellowship

Fire departments are a godsend when you need them. But fire departments only put out fires; they don't clean up afterwards. That's why Larry and Cheryl were lucky that Bonnie happened to be looking out her window the Sunday afternoon their apartment caught on fire. These three were members of the same Bible class. Bonnie started telephoning immediately when she saw what was happening at the apartment of her friends about a hundred yards away. And in less than half an hour, a crowd of people from the class were there, carrying furniture, washing off the greasy black film which had been left by the smoke, and salvaging personal belongings. By nightfall they had Larry and Cheryl comfortably situated in another apartment.

On a Saturday afternoon in early autumn one of the couples in the class were blessed with a new son. When their teacher arrived four hours later, five class members had already been there to see the mother, father, and baby. As the teacher left the hospital after a brief visit and a look in the new-baby nursery window, he ran into two more couples from the class, one of them carrying a beautiful cake shaped like a baby shoe.

They cared for one another. On hayrides they sang together. At seasonal parties they laughed together. When death took parents and other relatives, or when serious illness came, they prayed and wept together. And, when they met for Bible study each week, they learned together with eagerness and enthusiasm. Class sessions didn't bore them because they weren't bored with each other.

Christian fellowship and Bible study go hand in hand. Notice the striking combination of words in Acts 2:42: "And they devoted themselves to the apostles' teaching and fellowship, to the breaking of bread and the prayers" (RSV). Teaching, fellowship, breaking of bread, and prayers—important ingredients in the group-life of any Bible class. To neglect one of these functions is to weaken the rest of them. Teaching is the stackpole, the mainspring, the reason for a class's existence; but, when divorced from fellowship, personal relationship, and mutual prayer, it becomes cold and

sterile. Breaking bread together symbolizes intimate friendship; but bread-breaking alone does not create fellowship.

Fellowship is something more than glad handing, back-
slapping, and singing "happy birthday" songs to members.
Fellowship is a deep relationship, both personal and spiritual.
The New Testament term for fellowship, *koinonia,* denotes
"mutual participation." Thus, The New Testament speaks
of "the fellowship of ministering" (2 Cor. 8:4), "fellowship
in the gospel" (Phil. 1:5), and "the fellowship of his suffer-
ings" (Phil. 3:10); meaning, of course, that Christians "participate together" in all of these. In a true fellowship of learning
the members become channels of God's grace to one another, working together, "speaking the truth in love," and
extending mutual encouragement.

You can't manufacture fellowship by throwing class parties. Fellowship among Christians is born out of relationship
with the Master (1 John 1:3). But, given that basic relationship among the members of your class, there are things you
can do to enhance it.

If you are starting new, or if there has been a lot of turn-
over in the membership of your class, by all means have a
retreat. Getting away for a day or two at a lodge, camp-
ground, or even a home, will create a level of relationship
among members which might otherwise take months to
achieve. Let it be a time of spiritual emphasis, a time for
getting acquainted and for sharing mutual concerns. An
overnight retreat is best. But, if that isn't possible, make it
an all-day retreat, with the sharing of at least one common
meal.

A variety of social occasions will give your class members
a chance to know one another as persons, rather than as
mere faces in a classroom. Underscore the word *variety.*
Formal banquets are nice, but informal get-togethers pro-

vide more opportunity for personal conversation. And they are certainly less trouble. My wife and I would sometimes say to our class on Sunday morning (the couples class mentioned earlier), "We're having an informal drop-in at our house tonight after church. Come as you are. Bring the children and any cookies, cakes, pies, or potato chips you happen to have lying around. We'll furnish Cokes, hot chocolate, and coffee.

On one such occasion, our home began to resemble an Italian city bus at rush hour as class members and their friends streamed in. I don't know how many came that night, but all through the house there were clusters of young men and women, most of them sitting on the floor, caught up in intimate conversation. Also on the floor were small babes whose parents watched carefully to see that their little ones didn't get stepped on. It was a beautiful picture; beautiful because of what was happening. These people were sharing themselves with one another, deepening their fellowship as a band of learners in Christ.

The class was large; too large in some respects. It's very difficult for people to get to know one another in a large Bible class. We tried to overcome this difficulty by establishing subgroups of ten persons each. Sometimes, rather than have the whole class together for a social occasion, we would combine two groups for a dinner or dessert party. Next time around, the groups would rotate. Eventually, everyone had an opportunity to be with everyone else. One year, following this plan, the class had four simultaneous Christmas parties in the apartments of members. My wife and I dropped in on all four parties and ended up very full of fruitcake, candies, and other holiday dainties.

Another class in our city, faced with similar growing pains, helped members get acquainted with one another by pairing each couple with another couple for a full month. The understanding was that each pair of couples would arrange to be together at least weekly; eating Sunday dinners together, going out together, or visiting in each other's homes. After a month, these pairings would be rotated.

Fellowship also means mutual participation in prayer. In addition to times of corporate prayer in class, on retreats, and at fellowships, consider establishing a time each day when all class members will pause to pray about common concerns. Keep a "prayer log," a master list of objects of prayer shared within the class.

Personify Enthusiasm

One of the consistent findings of leadership theorists is that "groups tend to take on the characteristics of their leaders." A clear implication of this is that teachers must exemplify the enthusiasm they would like to see in their classes. There is something contagious about the spirit of a person who is genuinely excited about teaching the Bible. Unfortunately, there is also something contagious about the attitude of a teacher who looks upon it as a ponderous duty.

I once taught a seminary course which, to be truthful, didn't turn me on very much. The class was scheduled at the wrong time of day. The subject matter was not at the center of my interests. The students seemed to take a passive attitude. In short, the whole thing was something of a drag. But I made a valiant effort, dutifully preparing for class sessions and doing all the things a teacher was expected to do. When the students were asked to turn in a written course evaluation at the end of the term, a few were honest enough to write just what they had been observing for four months. "The professor didn't seem to be interested in the course."

I was stunned. How could they tell? I didn't know I had let it show that much!

But, friend, you'd better believe it. They can tell. If you go into your Bible class halfhearted and half-prepared, motivated primarily by the desire to "get it over with," your lack of enthusiasm will inevitably show.

Periodically, those of us who teach should look in the mirror and ask ourselves, "Are you really enjoying it? Are you truly excited about teaching the Scriptures?" If the answer is an unqualified yes, that's great. But what do we do about it if we find that our interest is waning?

First, we try to get at the causes of the problem. Sometimes you can find yourself going to class "like a quarry slave at night, scourged to his dungeon" (from "Thanatopsis") simply because you've gotten yourself too burdened down with demands on your time and energies. It occasionally becomes necessary to say no even to good things, when they keep us from giving our best to priority commitments. And Bible teaching is one of those tasks which demands high priority. It requires the "first-fruits" of a teacher's time. Too many competing responsibilities can soon take the joy out of teaching.

Superficial preparation can dampen one's enthusiasm. When I was in college, I often dreaded going to class on Monday mornings. That's because my weekends were devoted to pastoral work in a small country church, and I never got around to doing my homework for Monday mornings. I would go to class early enough to find a seat in the back of the room, putting as many people as possible between me and the professor. Then, relying on the adage, "out of sight, out of mind," I would slump down in my desk, hoping that I wouldn't be noticed during recitation time; for I had nothing to say. How different it was on other days when I had spent enough time in the books to be loaded with information. How eagerly I went to class, sitting toward the front of the room, even volunteering information if the professor failed to call on me. Teaching is a lot like that. What a difference it makes when you can go into class having done your homework well.

Depth Bible study is a never-failing source of enthusiasm for the teacher. In one of the world's great art galleries not long ago, I noticed how some people were dashing through each room, hardly slackening their pace, while others would sit gazing at a masterpiece, drinking in all its details. People approach the Bible in different ways, too. Some dash through a Scripture passage skimming ideas off the surface. Others grapple with the text, pondering its meaning, exploring parallel passages, consulting commentaries, saying to the Scriptures, as Jacob said to his mysterious opponent at Peniel, "I will not let you go, unless you bless me." The latter kind of Bible study can fill the teacher's mind and heart with gems of truth that are too exciting to keep.

A teacher's attitude toward class members has a powerful bearing on their performance in Bible-study sessions. The surest way to stifle participation is to approach class members with the assumption that they don't want to participate. Sociologists and educators have a theory which they call "self-fulfilling prophecy." Basically, the theory is that people will behave pretty much like someone expects them to behave. If a schoolteacher is convinced that her pupils are all "low-achievers," they will perform at a low level of achievement; but if a teacher has high expectations of the same class, their performance will be much better.

If a Bible teacher is convinced that her class members

"aren't interested in anything," that they will not prepare lessons or participate in class discussions, her teaching will be shaped by these expectations. Assuming that they have no information, she tells them everything. They, in turn, quit studying the lessons, because they know that the teacher will tell them everything. Assuming that they have nothing to say, she does all the talking. They, in turn, quit trying to say anything, because they are under the impression that the teacher prefers to do all the talking. When this pattern becomes entrenched in a class, it is difficult to change it.

An enthusiastic teacher will not always turn a lifeless class into a dynamic one, but an unenthusiastic teacher can readily turn a lively class into a dull one. In the long run, perhaps the most lasting contributions a teacher can make is to get a group of learners genuinely excited about Bible study. And such an attitude must be caught rather than taught; caught through the spirit of a teacher who honors the Bible, cherishes learners, and loves the challenge of teaching.

Get Class Members Involved

My friend and colleague, Allen W. Graves, once said, "No man is lazy, except in pursuit of another man's goals." What an important insight. You might be bored with my goals, but not if they are your goals, too. There is a limit to what you'll do to accomplish my purposes; but you will devote considerable time and energy to accomplishing *our* purposes.

A clear implication of this principle is that the Bible teacher should do everything possible to involve learners in planning and implementing Bible study activities, administering the affairs of the class, and carrying out class projects.

Involving learners in Bible study activities. A large class of single adults, a "college and career" group, were getting ready for a six-month study of Paul's letters to the Corinthians. The teacher assigned one chapter from 1 or 2 Corinthians to each individual and gave the following instructions: "I want you to read through your assigned chapter carefully. As you read, place an exclamation point in the margin of your Bible when you come across a significant idea; and if anything raises a question in your mind, identify this with a question mark."

It took about ten minutes for these individual assignments to be completed. Then the teacher organized the class into groups of five and gave these further instructions: "I would like for each person to share with your group the questions and significant ideas found in his or her assigned chapter. Then, on the large sheets of paper which I will give you, I want your group to list ideas and questions which you would like for us to explore in future study sessions."

After the groups had finished their lists, they taped these to the wall at the front of the room where everyone could see them. Then the teacher asked class members to indicate, by a showing of hands, the three ideas or questions out of all the lists which interested them most. She went down the lists, item by item, and recorded the number of "votes" for each item. Some of the items got a dozen votes, some five or six, and some none.

Armed with this information, the teacher met with a committee chosen from among the class members. Together they worked out a schedule of lessons for the next three months. These were then duplicated and handed out to members and prospective members. The schedule contained a variety of interesting topics, such as, "What Should Be Done About Immoral Church Members?" "How Christians Ought to Settle Fights," "Was Paul for or Against Marriage?" "What About Speaking in Tongues?" and "The

Greatest Thing in the World." This was much more appealing than a mere list of Scripture passages to be studied.

The important thing about this process was that every member had a chance to participate in the selection of study topics. And it gave the teacher a chance to "bone up" on questions raised by the class members long before they came up again in study sessions.

Did you notice that the initial schedule of lessons was for three months, even though the study of 1 and 2 Corinthians was to last for six months? This was because the teacher intended to involve the class in another planning session before completing the second half of the six-month schedule.

This procedure accomplished one other purpose. The quick survey of 1 and 2 Corinthians aroused interest in a number of issues which members were eager to resolve. During the small-group discussions they would get worked up over some question and ask the teacher, "What do you think about this?" The teacher would smile and say, "I'll try to deal with that when we study it a little later on." You can be sure that the members of the class were eagerly anticipating some of the lessons.

I have been describing one technique for getting class members involved in the Bible-study process. Another way to accomplish this is to pull learners into the actual presentation of the lesson by asking them to do special research and give reports. If the lesson is about the study of the Tower of Babel in Genesis 11, ask someone to bring a report on the "ziggurats" of ancient Babylon, the pyramid-like towers found by archaeologists in the very region where Babel was located. If the lesson is on Psalm 23, a report on sheepherding in Palestine would be in order. Sometimes you might even have three or four members present a panel discussion on topics related to the lesson.

When teachers ask the question, "How can I get my class members to participate in the lesson?" I advise them to build opportunities for participation into the lesson plan. Let's say that you want to raise the question, "Which is most important to a Christian's life—worship, ministry, or knowledge of the Scripture?" Instead of simply throwing the question out, organize the class into groups of three (it can be done in seconds) and ask each person to share an answer with the others in the group. You can also use pencil-and-paper exercises or brainstorming activities to encourage participation in class.

Let the people you teach know that you really mean it when you ask them to participate. Some learners have been conditioned through years of experience to believe that they are not really expected to take part in the lesson. In a small church in Indiana my wife and I sat in an adult Bible class taught by a man who, we were told, was a lay preacher. That helped me to understand why he taught the class as he did. He preached the lesson. At the breakfast table that morning, our hostess had advised us, "Don't worry about studying the lesson. You won't have a chance to say anything." And she was right. The teacher's presentation was strictly a monologue. He kept his face buried in his notes the whole time, coming up for air only once in a while, long enough to ask, "Any questions or comments?" But his class members had been trained very well. They knew by now that they weren't really supposed to respond to this question.

To convince class members that you really do want them to answer questions, you might have to "wait them out." It will be difficult to resist the temptation to answer your own questions, if no one responds immediately. If you wait until someone finally comes across with an answer, the silence can become very awkward; but class members will eventually catch on to the idea that you expect them to respond.

Involving members in the administration of class affairs.
I once administered a test to help members of a Bible class rate themselves. It was entitled, "What Kind of Class Member Am I?" One of the items on the test was, "Do I help arrange the chairs in our classroom, or do I just assume that someone else should wait on me?" That was a pointed question, I'll admit. But the test was designed to jostle individuals into thinking about such things. And it worked. One member said, "You know, it had never occurred to me that someone was spending time each week setting up our classroom, or that I could help. But I'd like to volunteer.

Some teachers are needlessly overworked; "needlessly," because help is available for the asking. Why should teachers of adults or youth arrange chairs, keep the room tidy, distribute materials, telephone absentees, plan class projects, pick up the ice for class socials, take care of records, or track down the missing lectern? Teachers need help with such tasks; but, more importantly, class members need to have these responsibilities. Personal involvement in the work of the class gives them a sense of ownership in the enterprise.

It wasn't by accident that Bonnie was able to muster so many class members the afternoon Larry's and Cheryl's apartment caught on fire. The class membership had been organized into groups. Each group had a couple designated as group leaders. Whenever we wanted to contact the entire membership by telephone, Bonnie simply called the group leaders and they called the members of their groups.

The group leaders had other duties. If anyone was absent

from a Bible-study session, the group leaders contacted them. Rarely was anyone absent without being accounted for within a day or two. The group leaders also served as "pastors" to the members of their groups; visiting them in sickness, comforting them in times of grief or distress, and helping the teacher stay abreast of these things.

This class organization was born one Saturday evening when my wife and I had three couples who seemed to be natural leaders over for dinner. After dinner we sat at the table, going through the class roll and forming groups according to geographical location within the city. Then we talked about potential leaders for the groups. That same evening, each prospective group leader was contacted and each agreed to accept the responsibilities mentioned above.

In addition to the group organization, we had three important committees; a membership committee, a social committee, and a ministry committee. The membership committee maintained records and gave careful attention to the integration of new members into the class. They were responsible for getting in touch with newcomers after their first visit to the class. The social committee planned monthly class get-togethers and provided coffee and tea at the beginning of each weekly session. The ministry committee coordinated ministry projects.

With nine groups and three committees, we had more than two dozen members involved in administrative responsibilities. And, beyond that, the three committees were always busy recruiting other class members for special responsibilities, such as leading ministry projects, providing refreshments, contacting newcomers, and entertaining at socials. Virtually everyone got into the game. There were few "bench-warmers" in the class. Thus, they really meant it when they spoke of "our" class.

TEACHING LAB ACTIVITY NO. 23

Instructions: Remember the self-rating test for class members mentioned earlier? I used one item from that test as an example. Read the three sample items below; then see if you can add seven items of your own. When you have finished this activity, you will have a useful self-rating test which you can administer to your own class members.

MY RATING IS:

Good   *Fair*   *Poor*

1. Do I take responsibility for making newcomers feel welcome; or do I leave that to others? ___ ___ ___

2. Do I help arrange the chairs in our classroom; or do I just assume that someone else should wait on me? ___ ___ ___

3. Do I listen carefully when others are speaking in class; or am I more interested in what I have to say? ___ ___ ___

4. ___ ___ ___

5. ___ ___ ___

6.   ___ ___ ___

7.   ___ ___ ___

8.   ___ ___ ___

9.   ___ ___ ___

10.   ___ ___ ___

(Just in case you had trouble thinking up seven more items, here are some ideas that might help: "Do I pray for my teacher? dominate the discussion? arrive early? prepare lesson? call up absentees? encourage those who don't say much?)

Involving members in class projects. Bible study should be something more than sharing words in weekly sessions. In Jesus, "the Word was made flesh." So often, in Bible study, the Word becomes just words. That is unfortunate, for Christian ministry is the natural outcome of Bible study. It is more than that, really; it is a part of the Bible-study process itself. Does one really understand the meaning of Jesus' words, "I was hungry and you gave me food . . . I was sick and you visited me . . . I was in prison and you came to me," without actually doing these things?

Our class took seriously the biblical injunction, "Be ye doers of the word, and not hearers only." Our members conducted services in the area nursing homes, served as counselors in medical agencies, helped with pastoral visitation in our church, and worked in children's homes. In addition, the class took on a special ministry project each month.

The group structure described earlier helped us carry out the pastoral visitation ministry. Our church's assistant pastor would give us a list of twenty to forty assignments each week. In less than five minutes, these could be divided among the group leaders, and they in turn would pass them on to members of their groups. During the following week, group leaders would receive reports on these visits. If members were slow about reporting, group leaders would give them a call.

I have said a great deal about a young adult class, since my most recent Bible teaching experience has been with such a group. But, no matter what the ages of your members, these ideas will work equally well. Older adult classes have a great time taking on projects such as serving refreshments daily at Vacation Bible School, serving as guides for visually handicapped persons on shopping trips, or "adopting" stu-

236 How to Teach the Bible

dents who are away from home. Middle-aged businessmen and professional women can perform a marvelous ministry by using their contacts to help youth find employment or by offering professional services on a voluntary basis to people who are in need.

There are other kinds of class projects, of course. A work party, where members come together to redecorate their classroom, can do a lot to strengthen fellowship. To paraphrase a saying, "Classes that paint together, stay together." It's easy to talk with people you have worked side by side with in paint-streaked blue jeans on Friday night.

Let me remind you that we are discussing ways to generate enthusiasm for Bible study. That is precisely what happens when your class members take the study of the Word seriously enough to do something about it. The study of Scripture is somewhat like the behavior of electric current. Electricity doesn't flow through a wire until it is used on the other end of the line. But, when it is put to use, it becomes a moving, energetic force. Similarly, Bible study takes on a dynamic quality when the hearers of the Word are acting upon it in practical ways.

TEACHING LAB ACTIVITY NO. 24

Instructions: This exercise is designed to help you expand your thinking about possible class projects in your own situation. Read the questions, then write down as many responses as possible. If you need more room, use an extra sheet of paper.

1. Read Matthew 25:35-36. Can you identify persons or groups in your community who fit each of the categories mentioned here? How could your class carry out a ministry to each of them?

- The hungry and thirsty:

- The stranger:

- The naked:

- The sick:

- The prisoner:

2. What services need to be performed within your church? What class projects could meet these needs?

3. What needs in the community could be met through class projects?

4. Are there special talents or resources within your class membership that would be especially suitable for ministry projects? List them.

5. Check any of the following that would make suitable projects for your class:

_____ Clean up the church or a portion of it.

_____ Provide companionship for children without parents.

_____ Provide companionship for older people who are alone in the world.

_____ Provide transportation for the elderly or the handicapped.

_____ Help process materials in the church library.

_____ Offer services to assist in pastoral visitation. (Sponsor workshop for training in pastoral visitation, for example, hospital visiting.)

_____ Help youth find part-time jobs.

_____ Conduct services at nursing homes.

_____ Conduct jail services.

_____ Provide modern English Bibles for children who have none.

_____ Paint-up and fix-up your classroom.

_____ Assist elderly couples with spring or fall cleaning.

_____ Provide homes-away-from-home for students.

_____ Help teachers of children visit their homes.

_____ Share highlights of Sunday School lesson with sick class members.

Magnify persons. A man of humble origin told me about attending a political rally at the county courthouse. The highlight of the afternoon for him was a fleeting personal encounter with the political orator who spoke at the rally. Holding out his hand and looking at it, he said, "Man, he shook that hand just like I was somebody!"

Everyone wants to be somebody, to be recognized as a person. Not as a digit in an attendance figure, not as a face in an audience, not as a warm body occupying a chair, but as a person. It's hard to be enthusiastic about Bible study where no one knows who you are.

Speaking to the people in your classroom by name is a simple thing. But it is one of the most meaningful things you can do. Where classes are large, or there hasn't been enough time for everyone to get acquainted, nametags will do a lot to add a personal dimension to the sessions.

You appreciate and care about your members. Let them know it by sending personal notes or telephoning on special occasions. Many people gather around to comfort a person at a time of sorrow, but only good friends take note of things like birthdays, anniversaries, promotions, special achievements, graduations within the family, and the births of grandchildren. The teacher ought to be one of those friends.

The Bible teacher should, by all means, respond to the crises which arise in the lives of members. There are limits to our time and energy, of course, and a volunteer teacher can hardly be a full-time pastor and counselor. But there are some crises which we dare not ignore without raising serious questions concerning our credibility as interpreters of a Book which exalts the themes of service and love.

On a bright, sunny day my wife and I stood in the heavy shadows of a hospital room where a lovely seventeen-year-old girl lay dying of cancer. She was near the end of a long struggle. Her mother was a member of my wife's Bible class. Very little was said. Words really weren't necessary, because these two women had talked many times about the painful web of circumstances which had brought us all to this room. There was understanding between them as spirit touched spirit. But a teacher does not achieve that level of communication with members through encounters in the classroom alone. It comes only by walking with them through their private vales of tears.

Even your style of teaching, your manner in the classroom, can magnify or minimize the value of persons. A teacher who is sensitive to the importance of every individual in the class will often say things like, "Bob, as a policeman you probably are well-equipped to understand the tension between God's mercy and divine justice; have you ever felt sorry for a person even though you knew he must pay the penalty for violating the law?" Or, "Mildred made an interesting point as we were talking after class last week. She said . . . ." Such a teacher recognizes persons, affirms them, lets them know that they have a worthwhile contribution to make.

On the other hand, you can squelch the enthusiasm of persons in many subtle ways. Pay no attention when they raise questions. Look at your watch when someone expresses an idea. Reply to contributions with a mere, "Uh-huh. Now as I was saying . . . ." If a member disagrees with you, overwhelm him with convincing argument. Speak only to your favorite members when you enter and leave the classroom. Direct questions only to the "star pupils" who always have answers. Ignore the members whom you do not know when you see them outside the classroom. In all these ways, a teacher can make individuals feel that they are less than persons.

No one magnified persons more than Jesus did. People

were milling about the sick man at the pool of Bethesda; but only Jesus helped him. Jesus was surrounded by admirers as he entered Jericho; but he focused his attention completely upon Zacchaeus, the most unpopular man in town. Lepers were social outcasts, feared and avoided by their countrymen; but Jesus touched them and healed them. A throng was pressing in on Jesus from every side, but he was acutely aware of the presence of a woman who could get close enough only to touch the hem of his garment. The Master Teacher walked among the crowds; but he ministered to individuals. And he is our supreme example.

Use Old-Fashioned Public Relations

Sometimes we overlook the obvious. Teachers who deplore the apparent lack of interest among class members could improve the situation a great deal by using some of the methods of the public-relations practitioner. Public relations is the art of maintaining good relations with your public through every means at your disposal. It would be more accurate to say "your publics"; for every organization has an internal public, made up of members, and an external public, consisting of those outside the organization. As the teacher of a Bible class, your concern will be primarily focused on your "internal public," your class members.

How do you communicate with class members? By telephone? Personal conversation? Cards and letters? Probably. But beyond these familiar media of communication, how else might it be done? The next teaching lab activity calls for some brainstorming on that subject.

TEACHING LAB ACTIVITY NO. 25

Instructions: Suppose you wanted to communicate with the members of your class for the purpose of arousing or maintaining their interest in Bible study activities or special class activities. In how many different ways might this be done? List below all the means of communication that you can think of. Don't stop after four or five. Use your imagination.

1. Telephone	11.
2. Letters	12.
3.	13.
4.	14.
5.	15.
6.	16.
7.	17.
8.	18.
9.	19.
10.	20.

Wait! Don't read this until you have finished your list above. Have you finished? OK. Did you include any of these ideas? (1) Posters inside and outside the classroom. (2) Printed stickers and badges. (3) Telephone chain. (4) Personal conversations before and after class. (5) Visits in members' homes. (6) Strip charts. (7) Mobiles. (8) Cassette recordings. (9) CB radio. (10) Class newsletter. (11) Announcements in class. (12) Handout posters or advertisements. (13) Dramatizations. (14) Photographs. (15) Postcards. (16) Pencil-and-paper surveys. (17) Specialty advertising items (such as imprinted pencils). (18) Newspaper ads. (19) Radio announcements. (20) Projected messages.

Communicate by every means. One secret of good PR (public relations) is to communicate through a variety of media. People tend to quit paying attention after awhile if they hear the same thing said in the same way too often. You can buy some very attractive cards to send to absentees from bookstores and mail-order publishing houses. But I've often wondered how a chronic absentee feels after receiving about twenty of these, telling him in one way or another, "We missed you in class Sunday!" But suppose a couple of your class members were to drop by with a piece of literature and say, "We're sorry you haven't been able to join us for Bible study recently, but we knew you would want to keep up with the lessons." That new approach would surely get the absentee's attention.

Some of the methods of communication mentioned in the teaching lab activity above will need additional explanation. Let's take a closer look.

1. *Posters.*—You plan to launch a study of the Ten Commandments in about four weeks. Your members walk into class and see a series of posters on the walls. The posters aren't elaborate. Each contains a single question, such as "And what are your favorite idols?" "Should Christians buy toothpaste on Sunday?" "What's wrong with cussin'?" "Is killing ever justified?" "Is looking, lusting?" "Does having much cause someone to have little?" "Are wanting and coveting the same thing?" After a week or two, you could add a line to each poster, "Don't miss our Bible study on   (date)   !"

A cardinal rule for using posters is to put them where they can be seen. Do your members and prospective members climb a certain stairway frequently? Put small posters on the stairs. Do they use a particular outside door? Place a poster there. Do they pick up their children in some specified location? That's the place for a poster.

Posters come in different shapes and sizes. They don't

have to fit a standard sheet of poster board. You can frame them, mount them on contrasting backgrounds, include three-dimensional objects in them, hang them or place them on easels. The most effective poster isn't too cluttered with information. The best ones contain short, pithy messages.

2. *Telephone.*—There are two ways to set up a "telephone chain." You can have a permanent one, like the one we implemented through our class organization. We could call our group leaders, and the group leaders would call the members of their groups; thus, contacting every member of the class. If you don't have a permanent structure like that, you can still use the telephone chain idea. Just divide the class roll into groups of six and select one person to call the rest of the people in each group. Give the callers the message you want to convey, preferably in writing (for example, "Our teacher asked me to remind you to bring your copy of *Good News for Modern Man* to class this week. We're beginning our study of Matthew, you know.")

3. *Cassette recordings.*—Small cassette recorders are so common now, some of your class members probably own one. A cassette recording is an excellent medium for communicating with absentee members. Just think how much it would mean to an individual recuperating from surgery to hear recorded greetings from fellow class members, or even an edited version of a class session. You can also use a cassette recorder right in the classroom. To promote the series of lessons on the Ten Commandments, play a recorded monologue in which Moses tells about his experience on Mount Sinai; or to kick off a study of Revelation, present a five-minute recorded message from a pastor or Bible professor on guidelines for interpreting this unusual book.

4. *Radio.*—Both of the suggestions pertaining to radio in the preceding teaching lab activity might have seemed far-

fetched. But there are areas of the country in which numerous automobiles are equipped with citizen's band (CB) radio units. Why not use this medium to get the word around concerning a class function? And a great many commercial radio stations have "bulletin board" programs on which they make announcements for religious groups and other organizations without charge.

5. *Announcements.*—Announcements in class sessions are a familiar medium of communication; so familiar, in fact, that they may easily be overdone. You can add variety to announcements, though, by putting on short skits or by enlisting the help of several members to put on a demonstration with hand-held posters. It's always a good idea to accompany an announcement with a visual of some kind. That way, you are appealing to eyes as well as to ears.

6. *Photography.*—What more effective way to stimulate interest in this year's annual class picnic than to put up a display of pictures showing scenes from last year's picnic? And what better way to introduce new members to the class than to put up photographs of them and their families along with other pertinent information? Photography is a versatile medium which has many uses. You might have a ten-minute presentation of color slides showing historic sites in the city of Rome to preview a study of Romans. (Slides of this kind are available from the audiovisual departments of many city or college libraries.) Or take pictures of everyone who attends a class retreat and send a print to each person involved as a keepsake. Maintain a bulletin board where members can display photos of vacations, picture postcards from members who are away, photos of new babies and grandchildren.

7. *Newsletter.*—You can't have a class newsletter unless someone is willing to pay the price. For it takes time and

energy to write, edit, print, and mail a newsletter. But it could be the most significant step toward building a sense of fellowship, stimulating interest in class activities, and keeping members in touch with the continuing Bible study program. A newsletter should be just that—news; a collection of news about members, former members, class events, and other items of interest.

8. *Pencil-and-paper surveys.*—Five minutes before the end of a class session, a teacher distributed slips of paper. The slips contained two questions: "(1) As compared to all of our class sessions over the past three months, would you rate today's session as better-than-average, just average, or below average in terms of its interest value for you? (2) What would have made this session better for you?"

Brief surveys of this kind accomplish at least two things. First, they say to your class members that their opinions are important to you. Second, they yield important clues for improving your teaching. They take so little time that you can afford to use them periodically; changing the questions each time, of course. Here are examples of other types of questions to use in mini-surveys of this kind:

(1) Assume that you are driving home with another class member after one of our sessions. You say: "Boy, that was a great Bible study session!" What would have happened to cause you to make a statement like that?

(2) On the days that we have our best class sessions, what takes place? On the days when we have our worst class sessions, what takes place?

(3) What did you like most about this session? What did you dislike most about this session?

(4) If you could change our class in some way, what changes would you make?

(5) If you could make some change in the approach to

teaching this class, what change would you like to make?

(6) What was the greatest value of this class session so far as you are concerned—the information acquired, the personal relationships, or the inspiration experiences? If you experienced none of these to a significant degree, why not?

(7) If a close friend were considering membership in this class, what reasons would you give him/her for joining or not joining?

If you do use such surveys, let class members know that you take them seriously. For example, you might occasionally say something like this: "Last week in our survey at the end of class, some of you suggested that . . . . and you will notice that I've tried to implement this suggestion in our session today."

Communicate—by all means.—At its best, good PR is not a bag of gimmicks to use on people; it is the art of using every means available to stay in touch with people. This means maintaining a steady flow of communication between teacher and members, and among the members themselves.

Ideally, a Bible class is more than an organization. It is an organism. The distinguishing characteristic of an organism is that its members are linked together in a living relationship. Paul pictured this concept beautifully in his description of a church as a living body. "As it is, there are many parts, yet one body. The eye cannot say to the hand, 'I have no need of you,' nor again the head to the feet, 'I have no need of you.' . . . If one member suffers, all suffer together; if one member is honored, all rejoice together" (1 Cor. 12:20-21,26, RSV).

What makes the members of an organism function as a unity? The answer is that they stay in continual communication with one another. The human body is bound together by a nervous system which has millions of impulses running

along its fibers daily. This communication system keeps all
the parts working together in perfect coordination. For instance, when you need to scratch your toe, your hand knows
exactly where to find the foot, even without depending upon
your eyes. When the members of the body get out of harmony with one another, the body is sick. And if a member
stays out of communication with the rest of the body long
enough, the member is dead.

I would not want to push this analogy too far; because,
after all, a Bible class is not literally a body. But it is an
organism. And organisms thrive on communication. This is
why it is most important for the teacher to stay in communication with members, and to help them keep in touch with
one another. If we describe a class as "dead," it may be
precisely because the flow of communication has ceased.

In practical terms, this means that the teacher will communicate with class members not only on a formal level, but
also on a personal level; not only in the classroom, but where
they live and work and play.

Think of the humblest person in your class; that quiet
person who doesn't say much, but who is always there. How
much it must mean to that sort of person for her teacher
to visit in her home and say, "I just wanted to drop in and
let you know, personally, how much your presence in our
Bible class means to me." And if you will work out a system
for doing this, it doesn't take as much additional time as
you might think. For instance, there was a man in a large
midwestern city who stopped for fifteen minutes in the home
of a different class member each day on his way home from
work.

Where members are widely scattered, the telephone provides a good way to stay in touch with members. But, again,
telephone contacts ought to be systemized. Maintaining a

"call list" and keeping a record of calls will help you to avoid the error of calling some members repeatedly and neglecting others.

Let the mail carrier help you stay in touch with members. Pen and paper can be a powerful medium of personal ministry. Don't assume that it's always necessary to write a full-blown letter when you communicate by mail. Write short notes like these:

• "Dear Bill: I know it hasn't been easy for you to be involved in such an extended strike at your plant. I just wanted you to know that you have been very much in my mind and prayers."

• "Dear Lillian: Remembering how it was when our nest was emptied three years ago, I have thought about you and prayed for you a great deal since John left for Michigan. It calls for a huge adjustment, but it can also be the doorway to an exciting new life-style."

• "Dear Ralph: How proud I was to read the article about your promotion in this morning's paper. Thought you might like to have another copy."

• "Dear Peggy: What you said in class yesterday about your experience with God during your hospitalization meant so much to me that I just had to sit down and write you a note this morning. Thanks so much for sharing such a personal and significant experience. God used you to bless the rest of us."

• "Dear Sandy: Thanks again for the beautiful job you did decorating our classroom last week. It's a wonderful thing to have a talent like yours; but it's even more wonderful that you are always so willing to share it with the rest of us."

• "Dear Harold: What does one say to a friend whose son has run away from home? It would be so easy to say the wrong thing, but much worse to say nothing. So let me just say that I care very much about the anxiety that you must be experiencing, and that you can count on my prayers and personal support."

• "Dear Louise: How wonderful it is to hear the news that you and Ed are grandparents. I always wondered how people could be so silly over grandchildren until it happened to us. Now I know. So, have fun being silly."

Such notes, short and to the point, can become channels of God's grace during significant times in the lives of your members. There will be occasions, of course, when longer letters will be in order. Sometimes the best way to deal with complicated problems, as in the case of a young woman who felt that her sister's suicide was an "unpardonable sin," is to put your thoughts on paper. But, usually a few words fitly chosen will find their marks in the hearts and minds of members.

Let Us Not Grow Weary

The primary concern of this chapter has been to deal with the problem of lethargy among members of Bible classes. As teachers, we also need to recognize that there are also limits to our own capacity for enthusiasm. We, too, suffer from the "tired blood" syndrome on occasion. The pressures of life can build up; attendance can go down; carefully laid plans can go awry; and people can disappoint us. When these things happen in massive combination, it's easy to lose heart. What do we do then? Where do we go to get our spiritual batteries recharged?

This question has many answers, I suppose. But, as I examine my own experience, there are three basic sources of personal and spiritual renewal which stand out above all the rest. They are personal Bible study, prayer, and people.

Earlier in this chapter, I mentioned the relationship between depth Bible study and the teacher's enthusiasm for the task. I want to give that nail another whack, because, in my opinion, it is one of the most important things that can be said to Bible teachers. You cannot teach the Bible successfully if you do not study it diligently. You must love it, live with it, understand it, and live by it, if you would teach it.

Some people insist that it is impossible to understand the Bible; they look upon it as a mysterious collection of ancient writings whose truths are locked up in cryptic symbolism. I strongly disagree with that point of view. The Bible is the record of God's self-disclosure, written in intelligible language by intelligent persons for intelligent readers. And its truths are available to anyone who will pay the price at the study desk under the guidance of the Spirit.

Making Bible study one of the integrating forces in your life will accomplish two purposes, both of which are important to your success as a teacher. First, you will understand the word which you try to communicate to others. But, secondly, it will be a continuing source of inspiration, revitalizing your spirit when it threatens to sag.

There's just one thing wrong with saying, "The Bible teacher ought to pray." It is so obviously true that we tend to take it for granted. It's like saying, "You need to breathe in order to keep on living." A self-evident truth. But how much conscious thought do you give to the process of breathing?

The teacher must become convinced that prayer is not just an "enrichment activity," not a mere "aid to teaching." It is the teacher's spiritual bloodstream. An international courier speaks with added assurance and authority when he can say, "Just this morning I spoke with the king." The same principle prevails when we presume to speak to God.

Personal relationships provide a third source of strength and vitality. The process of staying in communication with class members, mentioned earlier in this chapter, is not a one-way street. The teacher needs it as much as the members do. Seeing learners respond to the influence of scriptural teaching, sharing in their spiritual pilgrimages, and feeling the warmth of their friendship in the Lord is the real payoff for the faithful teacher.

Paul apparently knew that the task of the Christian workman would sometimes grow burdensome; for he wrote: "And let us not grow weary in well-doing, for in due season we shall reap, if we do not lose heart" (Gal. 6:9, RSV). That word of encouragement has meant a lot to me on more than one occasion. I don't believe we ever get to the point where we feel entirely adequate for the task to which God has called us. Sometimes I leave a teaching session elated over what took place; but there are times when I go away asking myself, "What went wrong?" The fire which you have carefully laid can sometimes smoulder and sputter rather than burst into flame. Those are the times when the words of the apostle help me to remember that the fruits of my teaching need not be measured by the outcome of a single session.

To Sum It Up

This chapter might have been entitled, "How to Keep from Boring Your Class Members." But that's too negative. It doesn't quite catch up what we've been talking about. We have been thinking about ways to make Bible study a stimulating, absorbing experience for teacher and learners.

As you have noted, this isn't a matter of employing gimmicks, making pep talks, and applying bandages to sagging morale. Enthusiasm isn't just an emotional "high," like the frenzy of basketball fans who have school spirit. The word itself comes from two Greek words, *en* (in) and *theos* (God). Thus, taken in its most literal sense, enthusiasm denotes the attitude of one who is "in God." This reminds me of what John, the author of Revelation, said about being "in the Spirit on the Lord's day" (Rev. 1:10).

Enthusiasm in Bible study has deep spiritual and personal roots. There are practical ways to bolster it—promotional tools, class organization, social events. But these are not ends within themselves. They are utilized to achieve the spiritual and personal values which generate enthusiasm.

The discussion revolved around five suggestions: (1) Enthusiasm for Bible study grows out of a genuine sense of fellowship among class members. (2) To build enthusiasm, a teacher must personify enthusiasm. (3) Involvement in the affairs of the class and in Bible study activities produces enthusiasm. (4) Interested members are members whose personal needs are being met. (5) Public relations techniques can maintain interest among class members.

I added a final word about the sources of personal and spiritual renewal for the teacher—Bible study, prayer, and personal relationships.

A Parting Word

The biblical message must be communicated. The Bible was not designed to become a museum piece, either in the archives of a library or on a living room coffee table. It was delivered to the people of God not to be preserved, enshrined, or carried about as a lucky charm. It was given in order that it might be shared. One who does not understand this has not fully grasped the nature of that message.

Teaching has always been an important vehicle for communicating the Word of God. "And now, O Israel, give heed to the statutes and the ordinances which I teach you," Moses said to the people (Deut. 4:1, RSV; 6:1). "And these words which I command you this day shall be upon your heart; and you shall teach them diligently to your children" (6:6-7, RSV; 11:19).

Jehoshaphat, one of Judah's godly kings, sent teachers out to instruct the people of the land in the law of the Lord. "And they taught in Judah, having the book of the law of the Lord with them; they went about through all the cities of Judah and taught among the people" (2 Chron. 17:7-9, RSV). The prophet Samuel and Ezra the scribe are representative of many religious leaders in Israel who conveyed the message of the Lord through teaching (1 Sam. 12:23; Ezra 7:10).

The most characteristic activity of Jesus during his earthly ministry was teaching. He "went about Galilee teaching in their synagogues" (Matt. 4:23; Luke 13:10). He performed miracles, but his miracles were often directly connected with his teaching (John 6:26 f.). He preached the good news of the kingdom, but his preaching and his teaching were woven together into a single fabric. What we call the Sermon on the Mount is prefaced by the words, "And he opened his mouth and taught them" (Matt. 5:2, RSV).

His disciples called him "Teacher" (Mark 5:35; John 1:38). People who stood outside that select band of followers called him Teacher (Matt. 8:19; John 3:2). And Jesus accepted that title, referring to himself as Teacher (John 13:13). It is significant that Luke, summing up the content of his gospel in the introduction to Acts, wrote: "In the first book, O Theophilus, I have dealt with all that Jesus began to do and *teach* (RSV, italics added).

When first-century Christians set out to communicate the divine message to a lost world, following the death and resurrection of their Lord, they adopted his methodology. They went forth teaching (Acts 2:42; 4:2,18; 17:2-3; 18:11,26; 28:31). The apostle Paul often spoke of teachers and teaching in his letters to the young churches (Rom. 12:7; 1 Cor. 12:28; Eph. 4:11; Gal. 6:6; 1 Tim. 3:2; 4:2,13,16; 2 Tim. 3:16; Titus 2:1,3).

Through succeeding centuries, the teaching of the Scriptures has been closely identified with the outward expansion of the gospel and the inner vitality of the church. During the Dark Ages, learning in the Western world went into eclipse and Bible knowledge was suppressed. The Scriptures were chained to pulpits and confined in cloistered monasteries. The message of the Bible became the exclusive property of the clergy, unavailable to the common man. And during those centuries the church languished in a state of spiritual lethargy and ineffectiveness. On the other hand, in those bright chapters of Christian history where the gospel has gone forth with power to reap a mighty harvest, and the cause of Christ on earth has flourished, teaching has always played a significant role in the lives of God's people.

As teachers of the Word, you and I have been called to a supremely important mission. Christian teaching is absolutely essential to the life of the church. Not merely helpful; not just beneficial. Essential! The church can no more exist without teaching than it can survive without preaching. This means that we must take our task with all the seriousness of a surgeon who prepares to make an incision in a living human body or an air traffic controller on whose instructions hang hundreds of lives.

But there is a difference between "conducting a class" and teaching, just as there is a difference between "filling a pulpit" and preaching. It is relatively easy to create the illusion of Bible study; it is more difficult to guide learners into personal encounters with the living Word. We can be satisfied with nothing less than that; for that is the goal of Bible teaching.

This calls for a high degree of commitment on the part of the Christian teacher. There is a price tag on the privilege of teaching. The teacher must pay the price of personal preparation at the study desk and spiritual preparation in the prayer closet. The cost must also be measured in terms of time and energy devoted to nurturing personal relationships. Christian teaching at its best is incarnational teaching. Even as the incarnate Christ entered into the world of human experience in order to reveal the mind of God, even so must the teacher enter into the experience of the learner in order to communicate the biblical message.

When one realizes the full significance of this calling, it is natural to shrink from it. On countless occasions, someone has come to me after a Bible-teaching conference and said, "If being a teacher is that big a job, I think I'd better resign."

I knew it was a jest; but often it was a serious jest.

If this book has left you feeling that way, let me remind you that God often uses hesitant servants in mighty ways. Look at Moses, one of the most significant figures in Old Testament history. When God spoke to him out of the burning bush at Mount Horeb, Moses said, "Oh, my Lord, send, I pray, some other person" (Ex. 4:13, RSV). When the divine call came to Jeremiah, he replied apologetically, "Ah, Lord God! Behold, I do not know how to speak, for I am only a youth" (Jer. 1:6, RSV).

As Solomon faced the awesome task of ruling Israel, he prayed, "And now, O Lord my God, thou has made thy servant king in place of David my father, although I am but a little child; I do not know how to go out or come in" (1 Kings 3:7, RSV). When the Lord called upon Gideon to deliver his nation out of the hands of marauding Midianites, Gideon protested, "Pray, Lord, how can I deliver Israel? Behold, my clan is the weakest in Manasseh, and I am the least in my family" (Judg. 6:15, RSV). Each felt his personal inadequacy; but each ultimately experienced God's sufficiency.

God doesn't insist that teachers of the Word be successful. He just asks that we be faithful. Some of the greatest joys that I have experienced in my own Christian pilgrimage have come out of Bible teaching experiences. But, on many occasions, I have left class sessions discouraged and disappointed, wondering why things had gone wrong. We never get to the point where we can guarantee results in our teaching; but we should never get to the point where we quit trying for results. A great preacher of an earlier generation voiced a formula which every Bible teacher should take to heart when he said: "Work as though everything depends upon you; pray as though everything depends upon God."

Appendix

The following lists of books will serve as a guide to further study in several areas of knowledge and skill related to the craft of Bible teaching. They have been arranged under several headings to make it easy for you to locate the books you need. I have included brief notations to let you know something about each book.

Knowing Learners Better

1. For teachers of adults.

Coleman, Lucien, *Understanding Adults* (Nashville: Convention Press, 1969). This inexpensive book examines many of the spiritual, psychological, and social needs of adult class members.

Dye, Harold, *No Rocking Chair for Me* (Nashville: Broadman Press, 1976). A very readable book on the problems of senior adults—compulsory retirement, the fear of retirement, economic pressures, and others.

Gray, Robert M. and Moberg, David *The Church and the Older Person* (Revised) (Grand Rapids: Wm. B. Eerdmans Publishing Co., 1977). If you teach older adults, this one will help you to gain valuable insights into the personal experiences of class members.

Knight, George W. and Steen, John W., *Plain Talk About Growing Old* (Nashville: Convention Press, 1977). Two experienced editors of periodicals for families and older adults talk about the nature of older adults.

Segler, Franklin M., *Alive! and Past 65!* (Nashville: Broadman Press, 1975). A personal testimony from one who has experienced retirement and all that goes with it. Written to help the aging understand themselves, this book is full of useful insights for the teacher of senior adults.

Sheehy, Gail, *Passages: Predictable Crises of Adult Life* (N. Y.: E. P. Dutton and Co., Inc., 1976). A best-selling book about the crises in the lives of young adults and middle-aged adults. Get the paperback edition; it's cheaper.

Wood, Britton, *Single Adults Want to Be the Church, Too* (Nashville: Broadman Press, 1977). A readable book, with plenty of helpful information for those who want to learn more about working with single adults.

2. For teachers of youth.

Garrison, Karl C., *Before You Teach Teenagers* (Philadelphia: Lutheran Church Press, 1962). This book is several years old, but it's still one of my favorite books on working with youth in Bible study.

Murphree, Garvice and Dorothy, *Understanding Youth* (Nashville: Convention Press, 1969). Written by a husband-wife team who are well-qualified to speak from experience, this is a good discussion of the needs and interests of youth. Inexpensive, too.

Sparkman, Temp, *Knowing and Helping Youth* (Nashville: Broadman Press, 1977). An impressive collection of experts in church youth work wrote this book; and it was edited by an experienced religious educator. An in-depth treatment of several aspects of the experience of youth.

Books to Help You in Your Bible Study

1. Concordances.

If I could have only one Bible study tool, my choice would be a large concordance like one of the following.

Cruden's Unabridged Concordance (Nashville: Broadman Press, n. d.). A complete concordance containing all the biblical words you'll ever want to look up.

Strong's Exhaustive Concordance of the Bible (New York: Abingdon Press, 1977). Every word of the Bible and all the passages in which they are found are treated in this concordance.

The Zondervan Expanded Concordance (Grand Rapids: Zondervan Publishing Co., 1968). This concordance is unique in that it includes key words from six modern Bible translations as well as the King James Version. If you like to use varied translations, you'll find this quite useful.

Young's Analytical Concordance to the Bible (Grand Rapids: Wm. B. Eerdmans Publishing Co., 1955). This happens to be the one that I use most. It is a very complete concordance with 311,000 references.

2. Bible Dictionaries and Encyclopedias.

Davis Dictionary of the Bible (Nashville: Broadman Press, n. d.). First published many years ago, this dictionary is now in its fourth edition, taking advantage of the latest biblical scholarship.

The Interpreter's Dictionary of the Bible (New York: Abingdon Press, 1962, 1976). This is actually a five-volume encyclopedia of the Bible offering a treasury of reliable, up-to-date information. I use my set repeatedly.

The New Harper's Bible Dictionary (New York: Harper and Row, Pub., 1973.) Unusually comprehensive for a one-volume dictionary. Quite up-to-date.

3. Bible Atlases.

Oxford Bible Atlas, Second Edition (New York: Oxford University Press, 1974). A very impressive atlas, with scholarly explanations of biblical geography and history as well as color maps and numerous photographs.

The Bible Atlas (Nashville: Broadman Press, 1975). This atlas has 26 colored maps, a number of black and white maps, and many photographs. These are arranged in the general order of the biblical narrative, from Genesis to Revelation.

The Zondervan Pictorial Bible Atlas (Grand Rapids: Zondervan Publishing Co., 1969). In addition to maps and pictures illustrating the geography of biblical times, the text gives you information about the people and cultures depicted in biblical events.

4. One-volume commentaries.

Black, Matthew, and Rowley, H. H., editors, *Peake's Commentary on the Bible* (New York: Thomas Nelson and Sons, 1962). Well-known and highly recommended, this commentary was written by 60 Bible scholars in Europe and America.

Guthrie, Donald, and J. A. Motyer, *The New Bible Commentary: Revised* (Grand Rapids: Wm. B. Eerdmans and Co., n. d.). A dependable commentary by conservative scholars.

Jamieson, Fausett, and Brown, *Commentary on the Whole Bible* (Grand Rapids: Zondervan Publishing Co., n. d.). An old reliable; a well-known commentary of good quality.

Laymon, Charles, editor, *The Interpreter's One Volume Commentary on the Whole Bible* (New York: Abingdon Press, 1971). A splendid commentary which meets the same high standards of scholarship as the larger multiple-volume *Interpreter's Bible.* Based on the Revised Standard Version text.

Neil, William, *Harper's Bible Commentary* (New York: Harper, 1971.) A well-written commentary of good quality. Not as detailed as much larger volumes, but has interesting interpretations.

Paschall, H. Franklin and Hobbs, Herschel H., editors, *The Teacher's Bible Commentary* (Nashville: Broadman Press,

1972). This commentary is unique in that it was designed especially to meet the needs of Sunday School teachers. It features not only interpretation of the text, but also applications of the Bible's truths to life today. Very readable and well-illustrated.

5. Multiple-volume commentaries.

Allen, Clifton J., editor *The Broadman Bible Commentary* (Nashville: Broadman Press, 1969-73). A happy combination of dependable Bible scholarship and readable style makes this an excellent all-purpose commentary for Bible teachers. When teachers want to buy their first set of commentaries, this is the one I recommend.

Barclay, William, *The Daily Study Bible, Revised Edition* (Philadelphia: Westminster Press, 1976). Easily one of the most popular New Testament commentaries in the English-speaking world. Literally millions of these volumes have been sold. Written in the "people's language," this commentary offers intriguing interpretations illustrated with hundreds of examples from classical literature.

Buttrick, George, general editor, *The Interpreter's Bible* (New York: Abingdon Press, 1952). A highly respected "standard" set of commentaries of excellent quality. Truly a wealth of information on the Bible and its interpretation.

Matthew Henry's Commentary on the Whole Bible (Old Tappan, N. J.: Fleming H. Revell, Co., 1960). An old standby, this commentary has been around for more than 250 years; but it is still widely used by teachers who like its readable style and conservative point-of-view.

Tasker, R. V. G., editor, *Tyndale New Testament Commentaries* (Grand Rapids: Wm. B. Eerdman's Co., n. d.). A popular set of New Testament commentaries written by conservative scholars. (As in the case of most multiple-volume sets, these volumes may be purchased separately.)

6. Special Bible-study helps.

Abingdon Bible Handbook (New York: Abingdon Press). A fascinating and useful compendium of information about the Bible, written on a fairly scholarly level.

Eerdman's Handbook to the Bible (Grand Rapids: Wm. B. Eerdman's and Co.). Another useful reference work. If you need to know something pertaining to the history or geography of the Bible, or various other kinds of information, chances are it'll be in this volume.

Halley's Bible Handbook (Revised) (Grand Rapids: Zondervan Publishing Co.). Probably one of the most popular volumes of this kind, this handbook has been used by generations of Bible students. It has been greatly improved by recent revision.

Revised by Callaway, Joseph, Adams, J. McKee *Biblical Backgrounds* (Nashville: Broadman Press, 1965). If you want a complete course in biblical history, geography, and archaeology, this is the book for you. Long used as a textbook in college Bible courses, this volume has been throughly updated recently.

Severance, W. M., *Pronunciation of Bible Names* (Nashville: Broadman Press, 1975). Here at last is an answer to an age-old problem in Bible study groups; a guide to managing those hard-to-pronounce names in the Bible.

Books About Teaching

1. Lesson Preparation.

Edge, Findley, *Teaching for Results* (Nashville: Broadman Press, 1954). The writer believes that weak teaching aims are one of the causes of ineffective teaching. He tells you how to write good aims and how to develop lesson plans on the basis of these aims.

Ford, LeRoy, *Design for Teaching and Training* (Nashville: Broadman Press, 1978). An ambitious treatment of lesson planning, this book deals with goal-setting, levels of learning, evaluation of learning, and procedures for putting lessons together. The volume is written in a step-by-step self-study format.

Sisemore, John T., *Blueprint for Teaching* (Nashville: Broadman Press, 1964). An easily understood guide to lesson preparation. Detailed guidance in the development of a lesson plan.

2. Teaching methods for adult classes.

Edge, Findley, *Helping the Teacher* (Nashville: Broadman Press, 1954). Excellent discussions of several well-known teaching methods and detailed instructions for using them effectively.

Leypoldt, Martha, *40 Ways to Teach in Groups* (Valley Forge: The Judson Press, 1967). Tells you how to use 40 specific methods in Bible learning groups.

Pierce, Rice A., *Leading Dynamic Bible Study* (Nashville: Broadman Press, 1976). This book emphasizes group participation techniques in Bible study.

Williams, James D., *Guiding Adults* (Nashville: Convention Press, 1969). A lot of help packed into a small, inexpensive volume. The writer discusses principles of adult learning and describes numerous specific teaching-learning methods.

3. Teaching methods for youth classes.

Burton, Janet, *Guiding Youth* (Nashville: Convention Press, 1969). A specialist in youth work for many years, the author shares from her experience a variety of teaching methods for use with youth study groups.

Dean, B. J., *Teaching Youth in Sunday School* (Nashville: Convention Press, 1977). A helpful discussion of teaching and learning in light of the needs and interests of youth.